T0240734

Financial Cybersecurity Risk Management

Leadership Perspectives and Guidance for Systems and Institutions

Paul Rohmeyer
Jennifer L. Bayuk

Foreword by Dr. Larry Ponemon

STEVENS INSTITUTE *of* TECHNOLOGY
THE INNOVATION UNIVERSITY

QUANTITATIVE
FINANCE
SERIES

Springer

Apress®

Financial Cybersecurity Risk Management: Leadership Perspectives and Guidance for Systems and Institutions

Paul Rohmeyer
Stevens Institute of Technology,
Hoboken, NJ, USA

Jennifer L. Bayuk
Stevens Institute of Technology,
Hoboken, NJ, USA

ISBN-13 (pbk): 978-1-4842-4193-6
https://doi.org/10.1007/978-1-4842-4194-3

ISBN-13 (electronic): 978-1-4842-4194-3

Library of Congress Control Number: 2018966187

Managing Director, Apress Media LLC: Welmoed Spahr
Acquisitions Editor: Susan McDermott
Development Editor: Laura Berendson
Coordinating Editor: Rita Fernando

Distributed to the book trade worldwide by Springer Science+Business Media New York, 233 Spring Street, 6th Floor, New York, NY 10013. Phone 1-800-SPRINGER, fax (201) 348-4505, e-mail orders-ny@springer-sbm.com, or visit www.springeronline.com. Apress Media, LLC is a California LLC and the sole member (owner) is Springer Science + Business Media Finance Inc (SSBM Finance Inc). SSBM Finance Inc is a **Delaware** corporation.

For information on translations, please e-mail rights@apress.com, or visit http://www.apress.com/rights-permissions.

Apress titles may be purchased in bulk for academic, corporate, or promotional use. eBook versions and licenses are also available for most titles. For more information, reference our Print and eBook Bulk Sales web page at http://www.apress.com/bulk-sales.

Any source code or other supplementary material referenced by the author in this book is available to readers on GitHub via the book's product page, located at www.apress.com/9781484241936. For more detailed information, please visit http://www.apress.com/source-code.

Printed on acid-free paper

This book is dedicated to all the technology risk managers in the financial industry, with whom the authors have utmost empathy.

Table of Contents

About the Authors

Paul Rohmeyer, PhD has extensive industry and academic experience in Information Systems Management, IT Audit, Information Security, Business Continuity Planning, and Vendor Management, among other areas. Paul is a faculty member in the School of Business at Stevens Institute of Technology and has presented and published on information security, decision-making, and business continuation. He has provided senior-level guidance to numerous financial institutions in the areas of risk management, information assurance, and network security over the past two decades.

Prior to his consulting career, Paul served as Director of IT for AXA Financial and Director of IT Architecture Planning for SAIC/Bellcore. Paul holds M.S. and Ph.D. degrees in Information Management from Stevens Institute of Technology, the MBA in Finance from St. Joseph's University, and the B.A. in Economics from Rutgers University. Paul has achieved the CGEIT (Certified in the Governance of Enterprise IT), PMP (Project Management Professional), and NSA-IAM (US National Security Agency Information Assurance Methodology) credentials.

Jennifer L. **Bayuk, PhD** is a Cybersecurity Due Diligence expert and CEO of Decision Framework Systems, Inc. She has been a Global Financial Services Technology Risk Management Officer, a Wall Street Chief Information Security Officer, a Big 4 Information Risk Management Consultant, a Manager of Information Technology Internal Audit, a Security Architect, a Bell Labs Security Software Engineer, a Professor of Systems Security Engineering, a Private Cybersecurity Investigator, and an Expert Witness. Jennifer is a cybersecurity risk management consultant and an adjunct professor at Stevens Institute of Technology.

Jennifer has numerous publications on information security management, information technology risk management, information security tools and techniques, cybersecurity forensics, technology-related privacy issues, audit of physical and information systems, security awareness education, and systems security metrics. She has Masters Degrees in Computer Science and Philosophy, and a PhD in Systems Engineering. Her certifications include CISSP, CISA, CISM, CGEIT, and a NJ State Private Investigator's License.

Series Editor's Foreword

The cliché about military planners—that they are always preparing to fight the last war—may apply to many of us in the financial industry as well. The financial crisis of the 2008 was driven by excessive leverage and dodgy asset valuations and so we focused on shoring up the banking industry through stronger regulation, expanded capital requirements, rigorous stress testing, and better valuation and risk modeling. But the risks being modeled are the traditional ones: credit, liquidity, market risk. And the stress testing concentrates on standard macroeconomic scenarios: recessions, oil price shocks, inflation, and the like.

But what if the risks that drive the next crisis come from a different direction? In particular, what if the next crisis is precipitated by a successful cyberattack on some key component of the financial system such as an attack that might take down a stock exchange or compromise a major bank or steal identities and financial assets on a large scale or an attack that might propagate at lightning speed across the globe, racing through markets that are now highly integrated and automated? Is this the next war that we are unprepared for?

There are plenty of red flags to suggest that this may be the case:

- It has been estimated that there are six new malware programs released every second (121 million per year)[1]

---

[1] Adam Janofksy, "How AI Can Help Stop Cyberattacks," *The Wall Street Journal*, September 19, 2018

- According to some sources, 40% of smart home appliances (cameras, DVRs, kitchen appliances) globally are currently compromised, and being used for botnet attacks[2]

- Even ultra-secure systems—such as a Boeing 757 aircraft—have been hacked, and could be "cyber-hijack-able"[3]

- There were over 300,000 unfilled cybersecurity jobs in the US in 2018, perhaps a symptom of unpreparedness[4]

In this threat-dense environment, even our vocabulary is disrupted. "User-friendly" becomes a synonym for "hacker-friendly" and a "network" becomes a channel for "contagion" and "secure" may now translate as "complacent."

Paul Rohmeyer and Jennifer Bayuk have written a book that should become a cornerstone for planners and decision makers in both the public and private sectors who are concerned with understanding and countering the vulnerabilities of the modern financial system. It is a timely initiative. Cybersecurity originally emerged as a discipline in the defense and national security field, but there is a growing concern that the financial system is perhaps at even greater risk from cyber crime, in part because it has evolved to be so much more open and interconnected in the very nature of its business models, and in part (as Willie Sutton, the bank robber, would say) because that is where the money is.

---

[2]Sarah Murray, "When Fridges Attack: Why Hackers Could Target the Grid," *The Financial Times*, October 17, 2018

[3]Peggy Hollinger, "Aircraft Face Remote Hijacking Risk," *The Financial Times,*October 17, 2018

[4]Janaki Chadha, "Wanted: Cybersecurity Skills," *The Wall Street Journal*, September 19, 2018

Financial Cybersecurity Risk Management is truly the first book to address this issue comprehensively. It is intended for a broad audience, to both introduce and characterize the evolving cyber threat matrix confronting our financial institutions, and to outline the principles of sound management for developing and deploying effective countermeasures. It will appeal, we hope, both to those involved in setting policy and to those responsible for implementation.

This is the second title in the Stevens Series in Quantitative Finance. Finance today is an industry in the throes of a technological and regulatory revolution which is transforming the capital markets, upending traditional business models, and rewriting the academic curriculum. It is an industry characterized by an expanding spectrum of risk, driven by technological changes that are engendering more dangerous "unknown unknowns" than ever before. It is an industry confronting the emergence of systemic phenomena—especially intensified network effects or "contagions"—that are the result of vastly increased levels of interconnectedness among automated agents in fully globalized electronic markets. It is an industry where everything is suddenly speeding up. The old manual markets and the old relationship-based networks have been displaced by high-tech, high-speed systems that threaten to outstrip our governance structures and management capabilities. Finance is an industry where up-to-date technical knowledge is more critical than ever. It is an industry in need of a new syllabus. The aim of this series is to supply the industry that syllabus.

For more than a decade, we at the Stevens Institute of Technology have been developing new academic programs to address the needs of the rapidly evolving field of quantitative finance. We have benefited from our location in the New York/New Jersey financial center, which has given us access to practitioners who are grappling directly with these changes and can help orient our curriculum to the real needs of the industry. We are convinced that this is one of those periods in history in which practice is leading theory. That is why the perspective of Paul Rohmeyer and Jennifer

Bayuk, who have spent many years working in this field before joining our faculty, is so valuable.

Working with Springer Nature and Apress, we are designing this series to project to the widest possible audience the curriculum and knowledge assets underlying the "new finance." The series audience includes practitioners working in the finance industry today and students and faculty involved in undergraduate and graduate finance programs. The audience also includes researchers, policymakers, analysts, consultants, and legal and accounting professionals engaged in developing and implementing new regulatory frameworks for the industry. It is an audience that is pragmatic in its motivation and that prizes clarity and accessibility in the treatment of potentially complex topics.

Our goal in this series is to bring the complexities of the financial system and it's supporting technologies into focus in a way that our audience will find practical, useful, and appealingly presented. The titles forthcoming in this series will range from highly specific skill set-oriented books aimed at mastering particular tools, techniques, or problems, to more comprehensive surveys of major fields, such as Rohmeyer and Bayuk provide in the present work for the field of financial cybersecurity. Some titles will meet the criteria for standard classroom textbooks. Others will be better suited as supplemental readings, foregoing the textbook paraphernalia of axioms, exercises, and problem sets in favor of a more efficient exposition of important practical issues. Some of these will focus on the messy interstices between different perspectives or disciplines within finance. Others will address broad trends, such as the rise of analytics, data science, and "large p, large n" statistics for dealing with high-dimension data (big data for financial applications). We also plan policy-oriented primers to translate complex topics into suitable guidance for regulators (and those being regulated). In short, we plan to be opportunistically versatile with respect to both topic and format, but always with the goal of publishing books that are accurate, accessible, high-quality, up-to-date, and useful for all the various segments of our industry audience.

A fertile dimension of our partnership with Springer Nature and Apress is the program for full electronic distribution of all titles through the industry-leading SpringerLink channel as well as all the major commercial e-book formats. In addition, some of the series titles will be coming out under the open-access model known as ApressOpen and will be available to everyone free of charge for unlimited e-book downloads. Like the finance industry, the publishing industry is undergoing its own tech-driven revolution, as traditional hardcopy print forms yield increasingly to digital media and open-source models. It is our joint intention with Springer Nature and Apress to respond vigorously and imaginatively to opportunities for innovative content distribution and for the widest dissemination enabled by the new technologies.

The Stevens Series in Quantitative Finance aspires to serve as a uniquely valuable resource for current and future practitioners of modern finance. To that end, I cordially invite you to send your comments, suggestions, and proposals to me at gcalhoun@stevens.edu, and I thank you in advance for your interest and support.

—George Calhoun
Program Director, Quantitative Finance
Stevens Institute of Technology

Foreword

A major deterrent to achieving a strong cybersecurity posture in the financial services industry is the inability to understand and manage the risk to critical systems and sensitive information. IT security leaders in financial services are keenly aware that recent well-publicized mega breaches and new cybersecurity regulations such as the New York State Department of Financial Services 23 NYCRR 500 are creating a sense of urgency among CEOs and boards of directors to address the threats facing their organizations.

Authored by Dr. Paul Rohmeyer, Program Director of the renowned Master of Science in Information Systems in the Stevens Institute of Technology School of Business, and Dr. Jennifer Bayuk, cybersecurity researcher and former cybersecurity executive, *Financial Cybersecurity Risk Management* offers valuable guidance on how to manage cybersecurity risk at the enterprise level. It is unique in its specific focus on the challenges financial organizations face, including those involving governance and culture.

The analysis begins with a thorough examination of the threat landscape in the financial services industry and the importance of understanding technology and human vulnerabilities. These vulnerabilities include the plethora of mobile devices in the workplace and the growing frequency and severity of Business E-mail Compromises (BEC). According to a recent Ponemon Institute study,[1] 79 percent of companies represented in the research say they certainly or likely experienced a serious data

---

[1]*Email Impersonation Attacks: A Clear & Present Danger,* conducted by Ponemon Institute and sponsored by Valimail, July 2018

breach or cyber attack during the past 12 months, such as phishing or business e-mail compromise. More than 53 percent of respondents in the study say it is very difficult to stop BECs.

Financial Cybersecurity Risk Management also discusses the consequences of data breaches when high-value assets are targeted. The findings from a Ponemon Institute study[2] are consistent with the authors' assessment that not safeguarding these assets will have serious consequences. According to the research, the cost to recover from an attack against high-value assets can average $6.8 million.

Once organizations understand their risk, the question posed is "How do I Manage This?" According to the authors, decision makers need to understand and communicate how technology supports strategy and how the enterprise governance function can help achieve a strong cybersecurity posture. *Financial Cybersecurity Risk Management* concludes with the potential cybersecurity implications created by new technologies that improve the customer experience and emerging standards that will result in increasing scrutiny of the financial services industry.

Given the mounting need to make cybersecurity a priority, *Financial Cybersecurity Risk Management* can be key to preparing financial organizations to think long-term and understand the investments they should be making in people, process, and technologies to prevent a catastrophic data breach or cyberattack. I strongly recommend *Financial Cybersecurity Risk Management* to IT and IT security professionals as well as to boards of directors and CEOs.

—Dr. Larry Ponemon
Chairman and Founder
Ponemon Institute

---

[2]*The Second Annual Study on the Cybersecurity Risk to Knowledge Assets*, conducted by Ponemon Institute and sponsored by Kilpatrick Townsend, April 2018

Acknowledgments

The authors would like to acknowledge the numerous colleagues, students, industry experts, and friends who provided countless hours of support and guidance in the creation of this book.

Dr. Rohmeyer would like to thank his wife, Jennifer Rohmeyer, and children, August, Terence, Leenie, and Gabriel, for their support and for politely enduring the always entertaining ad hoc exploration of cybersecurity risk management that frequently seems to come up throughout their many adventures.

Dr. Bayuk would like to acknowledge the constant support and encouragement of her husband, Michael Bayuk.

The authors would also like to thank Lori Ayres for wrestling through many complex requirements to create the excellent cartoons you will find throughout this book, and Jane Natoli for her diligent editing and helpful suggestions.

CHAPTER 1

What Are We Afraid Of?

The financial industry depends on the interconnection of institutions, markets, service providers, and customers that rely on a highly complex technology environment. The evolving characteristics of the global financial systems architecture drive an ever-expanding array of management challenges. Cybersecurity risk exists throughout the enterprise architecture in technology, personnel, and process domains, resulting in substantial risk management challenges. A variety of threats are evident and can exploit many aspects of the new complexity to gain access to critical systems and sensitive information.

Understanding the Threat Environment

This chapter examines the nature and extent of prevailing cybersecurity threats to financial institutions and markets. We are witnessing a truly global phenomenon that has manifested itself in several ways. It is apparent the relative level of skill, and motivation, of adversaries has improves substantiallu over the past several years, and the degree of sophistication of attacks continues to grow. There has been a rapid evolution of attacker tactics, with successive forms of attacks often improving upon earlier attack vectors. A detailed knowledge of the

© Paul Rohmeyer, Jennifer L. Bayuk 2019
P. Rohmeyer and J. L. Bayuk, *Financial Cybersecurity Risk Management*,
https://doi.org/10.1007/978-1-4842-4194-3_1

prevailing threat is essential to effective development of effective cybersecurity architecture. This knowledge should include understanding various types of threat actors and their respective motivations, as well as common tactics. An appreciation of threats is essential not only to defending against them but also to providing justification for funding adequate defenses. In-depth understanding of cybersecurity threats that are actually impacting institutions must be shared with business leaders to support and guide resource allocation decisions. It would not be unfair to observe that security solutions providers have presented have at times inflated fear, uncertainty, and doubt in efforts to sell products and services into the cybersecurity marketplace, perhaps leading to inflated skepticism on the part of business leaders. A mastery of threat concepts, and continuous monitoring of the threat landscape, may be helpful in convincing management of the present threat realities and need appropriate response.

Overview of the Risk Landscape

Cyber threats impact the organization as Operational Risk—risk that potentially results from, or impacts upon, control failures within any domain of enterprise architecture. This includes the chance for disruptions resulting from failed systems and processes, whether intentional or otherwise. Operational risk exists in all systems, processes, and financial activities and could ultimately lead to financial and other types of risk events. Enterprise Governance is expected to provide a platform to treat various aspects of Operational Risk; however, cybersecurity risk presents relatively unique characteristics that differentiate it from other types of operational challenges.

In the financial industry Operational Risk commonly involves technology, directly and indirectly. Direct risks include the potential for technical failures resulting from intentional or accidental misuse or from the manifestation of design flaws. Risk accrues indirectly due to an enterprise's reliance on deployed technology. Simply, enterprises that successfully deploy technical solutions will integrate the new technology into all facets of architecture; therefore, a sudden disruption to, or unavailability of, the technology could present adverse impacts. The nature of recent technical trends has presented unique risks. This includes the widespread consumerization of information technology via mobile devices. Mobility has resulted in new risks that could negatively impact as threats to confidentiality, integrity, and availability, essentially due to the portable nature of mobile devices and the chance for device theft or loss.

Understanding the Adversary

John Dowdy from Mckinsey observed there is a generally weak appreciation of cyber threats because there is inadequate information available about actual cyber attacks.[1] Historically, the lack of data has been attributed to the absence of detailed cyber information sharing from those who manage responses to cyber threats in both the government and the private sector. That is, although cyber-security professionals fully understand the extent of the threats, the general public sees very little specific and tangible evidence of immediate threats. Furthermore, the lack of threat information results in the systematic underestimation of the value of information assets at risk. This fundamental challenge of inadequate information creates uncertainty for those seeking to learn about the nature and magnitude of cyber threats. While the dearth of information should be expected to remain a challenge for some time to come, there is significant detail in the public domain that provides useful guidance on the nature of cyber attacks. So, while somewhat incomplete, the information that is available provides important clues to support an understanding of important threat characteristics.

Cyber threats can result from intentional or unintentional actions. Systems development and quality efforts generally are targeted to prevent or lessen the impact of unintentional threats, perhaps caused by unidentified system flaws or even user incompetence. Processes for identifying and responding to this type of threat are well-known and historically embedded into governance processes, including quality assurance, risk assessment, deployment of controls, and periodic controls testing. However, it is the intentional malicious actor, the so-called "hacker" that presents perhaps the most significant challenges to systems designers and owners. Malicious attackers are those who are focused on the theft or disruption of valuable organizational resources and, despite using similar tactics, may actually have very diverse motives, such as espionage or theft. We can refer to the individual or group that represents a deliberate, intentional cyber threat as an "adversary." The cyber adversary can be described in a number of ways.

One of the most important characteristics is the insider versus outsider perspective. Outsiders can arise from almost anywhere, operating with little or no specific knowledge of the enterprise. The adversary that operates from the inside of the organization, however, attempts to leverage a position of trust, having been granted some level of access to critical resources for a legitimate purpose. Once inside, they navigate the internal enterprise to gain resources they were never granted rights to access. Insiders present unique challenges, particularly within organizations that have chosen to emphasize the security of the external perimeter with relatively little monitoring of individuals after they succeed in passing through their initial security access path. The treatment options for insider threats generally orient around a combination of (1) enhanced screening at the time access is granted, and (2) ongoing monitoring of individuals and their movements (cyber as well as physical) within the architecture. These are not highly effective controls and so the degree of vulnerability to insiders is substantial in most organizations.

Another generally recognized threat characteristic is the typology of adversaries, sometimes referred to as threat actors. Individual actors include so-called "grey hats," which may at times violate laws and take atypical approaches in the course of investigating or attempting to improve security. There are also so-called black hats that are generally considered to have clearly malicious intentions and may employ decidedly unlawful tactics. The typology also includes groups that may have varying degrees of coordination. This includes criminal enterprises that seek financial gain, or perhaps influence that may be leveraged into eventual financial benefits. Political terrorist organizations may act to build support for, or demoralize the opposition to, a particular cause. This could potentially extend to state actors. Similarly, hacktivists may take action as a form of protest. Business organizations may present threats if, for example, they pursue information technology strategies to enable corporate espionage.

The Open Web Application Security Project (OWASP)[2] identified general attributes of threat actors—namely, skill level, motive, opportunity, and size. Variances in each attribute may cause the respective threat actor to prefer particular tactics or attack patterns. Skill levels can range from beginners that possess relatively low technical skills but possess sufficient competency to execute pre-defined, scripted attacks, up to the most experienced and skilled adversaries. Broad motives can vary widely, as described earlier, however drivers for individual attacks can be expected to emphasize short-term reward, as threat actors consider the short-term benefit of specific actions. Opportunities can vary widely, in consideration of factors such as resource availability and requirements, as well as access limitations. Finally, size is an important factor simply as a contributor to the scalability of the threat. For example, a similar threat level may be recognized from either a single, determined, or skilled adversary, compared to a large number of relatively unsophisticated attackers, such as in the case of an automated botnet.

Threat Categories for Financial Organizations

Common threats to financial institutions are visible by reviewing recent attack trends and breach events. Tactics will vary accordingly but the drivers behind breach attempts generally fall into one of three broad goals: theft of funds, theft of information, or cause disruption.

That's Where the Money Is–Theft of Funds

It seems like a week cannot go by without learning of another high-profile, high-dollar breach event that entailed the attempted theft of funds. The financial motivation behind such events makes them somewhat simple to understand–there have been robberies just about as long as there have been banks. It's the tactics that have changed with increased levels of technical sophistication and even innovation. However, the goal remains the same–to steal from where the money is. Funds can be sought for personal gain (the simple theft motive), but funds also may be sought in attempts to build increasingly powerful architectures to enable more robust attack capabilities.

As security controls have improved, the tactics of the adversary have adapted, employing direct as well as indirect methods. The classic "break-in," or hack, can be considered a direct attack method, where the criminal moves against a relatively visible weakness to gain access to networks, systems, and funds. Indirect attacks include tactics that may be relatively subtler, but of course seek the same end. This includes approaches facilitated by techniques such as social engineering, or e-mail phishing, where the attacker moves against an individual to essentially trick them into granting the attacker some level of access that is subsequently exploited.

There are numerous important aspects of indirect attacks to consider, including subtlety of actions as well as the attack duration. The subtlety of attacks is a result of the adversary taking small, measured steps that individually may not appear unusual. This reality renders common detection and control techniques somewhat useless unless the institution is able to make broad observations that enable it to group seemingly innocuous actions into a recognizable attack pattern. Simply, prevailing enterprise control environments have not been built to be effective in detecting or blocking such attacks. Similarly, the aspect of attack duration has become a concern with the emergence of the so-called "advanced persistent threat" (APT). A key distinction of APT is the adversary seeks to delay tactics, such as moving money, for a considerable period after gaining access. The period of delay can be used for such activities as detailed reconnaissance, the study of the flow of funds through enterprise financial systems, and selection of advantageous attack timing.

Information Is Power–Theft of Data

Information is present in many forms within every organization and can vary widely with respect to value. The value of information may generally be considered with respect to its criticality to the business as well as its sensitivity. However, information may be further characterized along a continuum of data, information, and knowledge that reflects variances in the meaning and relevance of information to the enterprise (Table 1-1).

Table 1-1. *Information Continuum*

Data	Information	Knowledge
External	Relevance	Internal
Explicit	Purpose	Tacit
Easily Copied	Business Context	Not Easily Copied or Observed

Observed facts and states of the world can be characterized as data. Data is generally explicit and lacks ambiguity. As described by Peter Drucker, data becomes information "when it is endowed with relevance and purpose."[3] Data applied to a specific business transaction, for example, becomes more meaningful. As information becomes further internalized to individuals and engrained in organizational culture, it increasingly may be characterized as knowledge. Proprietary designs, methods, market understanding, customer history, and other data that is part of deeper understandings of the organization and its environment are examples that may be considered knowledge.

There are numerous potential motivations for information theft, including enabling a subsequent theft of funds, disruption to the institution or individuals, or establishing capabilities for further information theft. Regardless of motive, threats represent potential attacks on value. Motivations for stealing information can vary but are typically acted upon with the intent to steal enterprise value for purposes of individual or competitive gains, as well as potentially disrupting the victim. Sometimes the data itself can have direct commercial value. In a well-known case from 2005, the owner of an investigations firm was found to have paid employees at numerous banks in exchange for customer information, apparently to establish a data resource to facilitate his completion of investigations for his paying clients.[4]

While the value of financial or physical assets is typically clear and quantifiable, the value of various forms of information is harder to measure.

Attackers may pursue data, such as consumer identities or details of specific transactions, or they may target information such as how customers may be using specific services or products and similarly may target knowledge such as capturing elements of intellectual property, including analytical models and observations of how such models may be used. Considering the information continuum further, we can envision tactics may differ considerably based on the attacker choosing to pursue data, information, or knowledge, respectively. So, while thefts of data may be enabled via direct attacks that seek to quickly remove data from the victim organization, stealing information and knowledge requires a longer, sustained campaign where the attacker observes not only data in motion but seeks to gain glimpses of how the data is being used. As mentioned previously, APT may be used to accomplish exactly that.

Information theft is unique when compared with thefts of other types of assets. A major cause of this uniqueness is tied to the fact information theft generally does not result in depriving the asset owner of the asset because the theft is generally executed as a data copy, or as action intended to deprive legitimate users from accessing the systems or data. In contrast, larcenies of physical assets do indeed take the subject asset away from the owner, depriving them of the asset's value. Consequently the characteristics of value loss with respect to information theft are not as directly observable as physical thefts. Simply put, if the owner of a brick and mortar retail store experienced a theft of inventory, they would be unable to execute their core business function until an adequate asset base was restored. However, the bank that has its customer information file copied by an attacker will still be able to function normally following the attack. In fact, it is possible the bank would not even notice they were breached, in contrast to the damage that is plainly visible to the victim of a physical asset theft. Furthermore, these unique aspects also create the potential information thefts may be visible to some in the organization, yet not disclosed to management, the board, nor customers.

Clogging Up the Works–Threats of Disruption

A wide range of attacker tactics may be employed to disrupt systems and/or data for the purpose of making the resource unavailable to intended system users. This includes highly sophisticated attack strategies such as building botnet environments that transform captive "drone" hosts into a formidable distributed attack force, as well as low-tech maneuvers such as power disconnects or even faux physical threats to personnel or property. The common goal of such attacks is organizational disruption, such as preventing customers from using services or stopping employees from executing normal job functions. In contrast, the reasons that adversaries seek disruption can vary considerably.

In a commercial setting, it is logical to consider that competitor organizations may pose threats to other market participants. The Knight Capital incident wherein a runaway trading algorithm sent a stock price plummeting was at first thought by many to be an intentional cyber attack. Planned strategically, such market disruptions could render the competition incapable of delivering goods and/or services, and such events could have short and long-term impacts, respectively. From a short-term perspective, if a customer is unable to buy from a competitor, there is at least a chance they may choose to purchase from the enterprise that caused the disruption. An important, although less immediate, benefit is disruptive attacks may damage the competitor's reputation, as they are unable to respond to potential buyers. Disruption may also be a tactic used to facilitate extortion and other demands for ransom payments. Business enterprises may find themselves faced with economic decision-making that leads them to pay ransom payments to avoid short- and long-term business disruption, thereby minimizing the impact of a system breach.

From within the enterprise, a devious or perhaps disgruntled insider may trigger disruption. An attacker that manages to first gain inside access to systems and data resources may find themselves in a position advantageous to the launching of a disruptive attack for extortion or ransom. Insiders may also present particularly severe challenges when taking negative actions as a response of some change in mood or attitude, perhaps driving them toward retribution. In July 2016, an agitated employee in a critical Citibank data center was sentenced to 21 months in federal prison for intentionally deleting router configuration information, causing widespread network disruption. The incident was apparently triggered when the employee received a poor performance review.[5] Political and social activism may be drivers of efforts to disrupt. It was reported in May 2016 that the website of the Bank of Greece was attacked by the group Anonymous because of "financial corruption."[6] Similarly, potentially higher impact threats may emanate from nation/state actors that have motivations to cause disruptions to perceived adversaries and rivals.

There are other potential motivators that should be considered. Attackers may seek to use a disruptive attack as a deception, drawing attention and resources to one apparent incident while simultaneously executing a separate, higher impact, attack. The adversary may also choose to use the deceptive distraction to enable intensive reconnaissance that might otherwise be detected. Finally, the possibility of experimentation should be considered as well. It should not be a surprise to find attackers executing a variety of approaches to leveraging the Internet of Things, for example, to increase their knowledge base and leverage it into novel attacks.

Facing the Threats

Cyber threats to financial organizations are complex, diverse, and potentially high-impact, calling for in-depth analysis to form the basis of enterprise cybersecurity policies, operational plans, and ultimately strategies. Threat modeling can form the basis for a comprehensive approach to the continuous identification and periodic reassessment of prevailing threat characteristics.

Two programs are essential for any organization to even have a chance at responding to the realities of the cyber threat environment: threat intelligence and threat modeling. Threat intelligence is the gathering of information about prevailing cyber concerns and activities, including insights on events, tactics, and potential response mechanisms. It represents the external perspective, to provide the enterprise with the ability to observe cyber events and activities outside of enterprise boundaries. The second program, threat modeling, is intended to apply potential threat scenarios to the organization's environment. Plausible threat scenarios can be identified by threat intelligence, of course, but also from the organization's own observations about breaches and breach attempts, and perhaps observations of data regarding attempted attacks. The organization may also draw insights from observing unsuccessful tactics of likely adversaries, perhaps hinting at future targets and tactics.

Threat Intelligence

There are many potentially valuable channels of threat intelligence that are considered "open source" (OSINT). This includes published research reports, media reporting, web pages, blogs, videos, and other readily available information. The promise of OSINT is its relatively high availability and ease of access. The challenge, however, comes from volume. In the current age of streaming "big data," this problem has become substantial, as the degree of resource requirements associated with monitoring of open sources has increased. The growing body of information embedded in social media systems has caused the creation of a new type of OSINT, referred to as social media intelligence (SOCMINT). SOCMINT presents high potential value as threat intelligence because postings may provide important aspects of context and description that add richness to the base of threat data. For example, an adversary that posts about their tactics, technology, and operational goals may provide security analysts value clues that can be used as the basis for improved controls and countermeasures. The challenge, however, remains with the substantial data volume that is continuously updating. There are methods and tools emerging, however, to help navigate and refine open source data, including advanced analytical capabilities as well as third-party services that sift through large quantities of potential threat information before presenting insights germane to the enterprise.

Threat Modeling

Threat modeling activities begin with identification of the organization's most valuable enterprise system and information resources, usually referred to as assets. Numerous resource attributes should be identified, including their respective forms, such as paper or electronic. There should be identification of the location of the resources, with respect to the devices and/or storage facilities, as well as the respective geographic location. Once the inventory, and nature, of system and information assets has been assembled, the organization should conduct interactive workshops to identify and consider various attack vectors that reflect the current architectural attributes, such as the network perimeter, applications, identity and authentication systems, and device configuration, among other factors. It is important to consider architecture at the enterprise level, to include aspects of the human dimension (such as systems users, connected partners, and support personnel) and the business operations process architecture in addition to the technical architecture to enable as complete an understanding as possible of the location and nature of information assets both in motion and at rest, as well as systems infrastructure—no small task in any organization.

As noted by researchers at Sandia National Laboratories, "Threats are generally much easier to list than to describe, and much easier to describe than to measure. As a result, many organizations list threats. Fewer describe them in useful terms, and still fewer measure them in meaningful ways."[7] Part of the challenge may be attributable to the relative complexity of threats, but also may be due to a general lack of understanding of the threat fundamentals described earlier (Figure 1-1). The Sandia report breaks down core threat characteristics into a practical framework that identifies threat attributes related to the commitment and resource base of the adversary. Commitment can be observed by the intensity or persistence, the use of stealth, and time dedicated to planning or executing the attack. Resource attributes include the availability and skill of technical personnel, knowledge, and access. Threat multipliers are also identified and include factors such as access to funds, assets to support attack programs, and the technology base. The attributes can be directly or indirectly observed and, therefore, can form the basis of threat metrics that should improve the quality, and usefulness, of threat models.

Figure 1-1. *Cyber threats*

Implementation

NIST draft standard SP 800-154, Guide to Data-Centric System Threat Modeling,[8] provides a foundation for an enterprise threat modeling program that is focused on the security of data resources. The guide outlines the following steps:

1. **Identify and Characterize the System and Data of Interest**. Each data element should be described in detail. This should include a summary of the nature of the data "at rest," including a description of the databases and host systems where it is stored. Some indication of how the data exists in host members during processing should be described. Similarly, the model should describe the data as it is "in transit," indicating the potential avenues the data may be transmitted within and outside the enterprise. Additionally there should be description of the data inflow mechanisms, including integrations from predecessor systems as well as device/keyboard data entry. The outcome should be a description of how the data flows through the system, a sense of the security goals, and insights on the authorized users.

2. **Identify and Select the Attack Vectors to be Included in the Model.** An attack vector is the potential path an adversary may take against a system. The universe of potential vectors is enormous, and so it is vital to identify plausible attack vectors to be included in the modeling exercise. This is where the value of threat intelligence begins to emerge, as past attack

histories and potential insights on tactics and motivations noted within SOCMINT can be very helpful in building a reasonable array of potential attack paths.

3. **Characterize the Security Controls for Mitigating the Attack Vectors**. The next step is matching implemented risk treatments against the identified vectors. Risk may be treated by the introduction of controls to lessen the chance of an event or to reduce its impact, transfer of risk to another party such as through cyber insurance, avoidance via architectural decisions, or acceptance where the enterprise has recognized risk but has chosen to move forward with a plan despite potential negative results. The outcome of this step is the identification of all deployed risk treatments taken against every attack vector.

4. **Analyze the Threat Model**. The final step of this exercise can be considered a form of "gap analysis" that reveals attack vectors that have not been adequately treated and therefore require attention. Instances of inadequate risk treatment may be obvious, such as when the organization finds an attack vector present risk that is simply not accounted for. However, in most cases controls are deployed, and so the analysis becomes increasingly complex in the attempt to estimate if the deployed treatments are sufficient, or effective. Assigning severity scores, or weights, to the attack vectors and similarly rating the risk treatments, can accomplish this. Ideally the analysis takes quantitative as well as qualitative perspectives.

Threat modeling as described in the NIST standard is very consistent with traditional approaches to risk assessment. However, the critical difference in the threat analysis is that it is based on consideration of very specific attack scenarios that have actually occurred, or are deemed very likely. Whereas traditional risk assessment can look to general threats, such as the threat of a breach, threat assessment brings the analysis to a deeper level of analysis and the granularity of the approach. This enables a more realistic assessment of the risk treatment choices the enterprise has made.

Moving Ahead

It's apparent the cybersecurity risk management challenge for financial institutions is substantial and complex. In comparing threat modeling to traditional approaches to risk assessment it is crucial to consider the fundamental differences between threat and risk. As described by the RAND organization, threats represent actors that may elect to act in a way that meets their strategic objectives. A risk, on the other hand, incorporates estimates of system vulnerability and potential consequences.[9] The outcome of threat modeling should provide a means for the organization to answer the fundamental question of whether they have deployed controls that may be expected to effectively reduce the risk to an acceptable residual level.

The upcoming chapters will build upon the risk-based approach to analyze the scope, nature, and breadth of current challenges. Chapter 2 begins the process with an exploration of potential cybersecurity weaknesses by considering where organizations may be vulnerable.

Notes

1. Dowdy, J. (2012) *Securing Cyberspace: A New Domain for National Security*, Chapter 5 The Cybersecurity Threat to U.S. Growth and Prosperity. (Washington, DC: The Aspen Institute, 2012). `https://www.jstor.org/stable/j.ctt19x3h93`.

2. OWASP (2017) OWASP Risk Rating Methodology. `https://www.owasp.org/index.php/OWASP_Risk_Rating_Methodology`.

3. Drucker, P. (1988) The Coming of the New Organization. *Harvard Business Review*. Harvard University. January-February 1988, pp. 45-53

4. Marlin, S. (2005) "Former Bank Employees Are Charged In Data Heist." InformationWeek. `http://www.informationweek.com/former-bank-employees-are-charged-in-data-heist/d/d-id/1032976?`

5. DOJ (2016) "Former Citibank Employee Sentenced to 21 Months in Federal Prison for Causing Intentional Damage to a Protected Computer." `https://www.justice.gov/usao-ndtx/pr/former-citibank-employee-sentenced-21-months-federal-prison-causing-intentional-damage`

6. Uzonovic, A. (2016) "Anonymous Target Bank of Greece Website with Massive DDoS Attack." `https://www.hackread.com/anonymous-ddos-attack-bank-greece-website-down/`

7.   Mateski, M., et al. (2012) Cyber Threat Metrics. SANDIA REPORT SAND2012-2427. Unlimited Release. Printed March 2012.

8.   Souppaya, Scarfone (2016) NIST SP 800-154 Guide to Data-Centric System Threat Modeling. National Institute of Standards and Technology. U.S. Department of Commerce.

9.   Neil Robinson, Luke Gribbon, Veronika Horvath, Robertson *Cyber-security threat characterization – A rapid comparative analysis.* (Cambridge: Rand Europe, 2013).

CHAPTER 2

Where Are We Vulnerable?

Risk is present in all systems. It is a naturally occurring characteristic of any innovative venture and therefore should be anticipated before, during, and after a new system is developed. Common points of vulnerability are visible in financial systems, and organizations can apply a range of methods and techniques to identify risk, begin the process of risk treatment, and understand potential outcomes. Risk exists in all aspects of financial systems architecture, including deployed technologies, the enterprise process architecture, and personnel. Interconnectedness creates new vulnerabilities and establishes the potential for cascading impact across connected enterprises.

Cybersecurity Weaknesses

Vulnerability assessment is the starting point in determining the nature and degree of system vulnerabilities and can take a variety of forms based on factors such as the balance of technological and non-technological concerns. The posture of any particular vulnerability assessment should be expected to reflect the unique nature of the subject system. Considering the term "system" in the broadest sense reflects technical, process, and human dimensions. Factors such as the relative sophistication of deployed

© Paul Rohmeyer, Jennifer L. Bayuk 2019
P. Rohmeyer and J. L. Bayuk, *Financial Cybersecurity Risk Management*,
https://doi.org/10.1007/978-1-4842-4194-3_2

technology, degree of process innovation, or support of emerging technology frameworks all should ideally have a strong influence on the scope of any vulnerability assessment.

Technology Vulnerabilities

The cybersecurity threat landscape is constantly shifting as adversaries find ways to exploit known technical vulnerabilities as well as discover previously unknown flaws. Vulnerabilities, including those that have not yet been discovered, exist in all technologies. One of the most important variables to consider is time. The following is an overview of the general timeline of the Vulnerability Life Cycle in technologies:

1. Vulnerability is discovered. Somebody, somewhere identifies a flaw in a system.

2. Exploit code is developed. Custom software is developed that enables or demonstrates a security breach via the flaw.

3. Exploit code is deployed. The custom software is delivered to target systems.

4. Vulnerability is exploited. The new exploit code is executed and succeeds in breaching the target.

5. Exploit is noticed by target. Somehow the victim (user or vendor) figures out they've been attacked and starts an investigation. Awareness of the new vulnerability often begins to become publicly visible at this stage, to both potential adversaries and victims.

6. Attack signature is identified. Observable attack patterns are identified and modeled into intrusion detection and anti-malware systems.

7. Fix is developed. A method for correcting the flaw within the respective system is engineered, typically using a software patch, configuration change, or some combination of both.

8. Fix is deployed. The corrected software is installed (i.e., patch is applied) to all instances of the vulnerable system.

9. Automated scanning enabled. Vulnerability scanning software tools are updated and periodically re-executed to detect uncorrected instances of the flaw.

There is an undetermined time gap between stages, thereby enabling detection via direct observation, including vulnerability enumeration and analysis. The cycle begins when a system flaw is discovered. Once vulnerability becomes known, it is only a matter of time before adversaries develop "exploit" code to take advantage of the newly recognized flaw. That means if the adversary discovers the flaw and deploys an attack exploit before the system manufacturer or user even knows the flaw exists, the adversary would potentially have undetected, and unchallenged, access to the user's systems. Such a scenario has been described as a "zero day" attack. However, if the technology manufacturer discovers the flaw before adversaries or the general public, a technical correction such as a software patch could be developed before an adversary can act. System users would need to apply the patch, of course, in order to thwart the attacker.

Attackers, therefore, are presented with two types of opportunities for successful intrusion. The first is the zero day attack, when unsuspecting users have no way to prepare for, or even recognize, the attacker's tactics. The second type of opportunity arises when system users do not take swift action to correct their systems even though the manufacturer has recognized the flaw and made corrective code available.

The Cyber Kill Chain as described by Lockheed Martin identifies very similar stages in characterizing Advanced Persistent Threats:[1]

1. Reconnaissance: Adversary scans target environment to identify vulnerabilities.

2. Weaponization: Adversary creates malicious code customized for target weaknesses.

3. Delivery: Adversary delivers the malware into target network.

4. Exploitation: The malware executes internally according to adversary plan.

5. Installation: The malware roots itself in the target environment.

6. Command and Control: The malware communicates with the adversary's systems.

7. Action on Objectives: The malware achieves the adversary goal, such as data exfiltration.

The fundamental difference between the models presented here illustrates an important characteristic of the vulnerability landscape. The Cyber Kill Chain describes the *purposeful targeting* of a specific victim that is characteristic of the Advanced Persistent Threat. It reflects the unique actions taken against the identified target, while the Vulnerability Life

Cycle as outlined earlier reflects the more opportunistic, *non-targeted* nature of the general environment. The Vulnerability Life Cycle reflects an emergent flow of events as newly discovered flaws are socialized among adversaries who subsequently seek to execute the new tactics against a range of targets of opportunity that can be observed vulnerable to the emerging attack.

Another key difference is the Cyber Kill Chain characterizes vulnerability discovery and exploit development (weaponization) performed by a highly skilled, determined adversary, while the generalized Vulnerability Discovery reflects adversaries will apply new exploits in a more opportunistic manner, across a range of available and potentially attractive targets. That means the potential for exploiting the generalized Vulnerability Lifecycle is available to even low-skilled adversaries. As a result we can probably expect many attacks against financial systems will essentially be "copy-cat" attempts (repeats of prior successful attacks) against targets of opportunity. This highlights a need, and opportunity, for prompt corrective action before a "lucky" adversary discovers a known vulnerability exists in a target of opportunity.

The 2017 Equifax Breach demonstrated that the acceptable timeframe to correct publicly known vulnerabilities is short and probably shrinking. It also showcased just how vexing the problem of managing software vulnerabilities is. The following commentary was posted by the Apache Project Management Committee (PMC) to the Apache.org website following the breach:

> We as the Apache Struts PMC want to make clear that the development team puts enormous efforts in securing and hardening the software we produce, and fixing problems whenever they come to our attention. In alignment with the Apache security policies, once we get notified of a possible security issue, we privately work with the

reporting entity to reproduce and fix the problem and roll out a new release hardened against the found vulnerability. We then publicly announce the problem description and how to fix it. Even if exploit code is known to us, we try to hold back this information for several weeks to give Struts Framework users as much time as possible to patch their software products before exploits will pop up in the wild. However, since vulnerability detection and exploitation has become a professional business, it is and always will be likely that attacks will occur even before we fully disclose the attack vectors, by reverse engineering the code that fixes the vulnerability in question or by scanning for yet unknown vulnerabilities.[2]

There certainly are a range of vulnerability management technologies to help organizations grapple with the complexities of tracking the never-ending cycle of vulnerability disclosure and exploit. However, cases such as Equifax demonstrate the technical complexities while suggesting tools alone will not solve the problem, and that means vulnerability management needs to be approached in a consistent and comprehensive way that leverages all elements of enterprise architecture, including people and processes in addition to technologies (Figure 2-1).

Figure 2-1. *Software updates*

New Technologies

Innovation is a common driver of technology projects. As such, just about all projects contain some risk from the usage of new technologies, changes to installed technologies, organizational modifications, and/ or some combination of all three. When we deploy technologies and methods that are new to the world, or at least new to us, we open the organization to potential adverse effects–we add vulnerabilities to our environment. Often the push toward new technology deployment is fueled by the promise of competitive business advantage, sometimes leading organizations to deploy new technologies before the associated risks are fully understood.

Geoffrey Moore has described the common technology adoption life cycle. Moore observed the technology adoption process begins with leading edge innovators and visionaries who act quickly to integrate emerging technologies. After a period of uncertainty and delay, referred to as the "chasm," new technology adoption is then caught up in a tornado of excitement and exuberant deployment, leading to broad acceptance. As a result, Moore noted, the new technology makes its way to "Main Street," a phase of widespread adoption, ultimately achieving total assimilation as remaining late adopters fall into line with the general population.[3]

We can view Moore's theory of technology adoption through the lens of risk, thereby providing a glimpse of new technology's influence in cybersecurity. Innovators and visionaries know they are accepting relatively high levels of risks for their early adoption, and willingly do so in the hope of achieving advantages in the marketplace. Other organizations may recognize the promises of the new technology but, because of their respective risk appetites, will wait until uncertainties in various elements of adoption begin to subside. In other words, risk plays a role in Moore's concept of crossing the chasm. So, apart from the functional characteristics, the recognition of available, effective risk treatments related to particular emerging technologies is a key limiting factor in the drive toward competitive business advantage. The tornado of adoption can begin once risk can be determined to be treatable.

Cybersecurity is thus a key component in the new technology adoption cycle, and eager business managers know they cannot proceed without an understanding of the emerging risk dimensions of the new tech. Furthermore, the risk dimensions of the new tech must be considered in light of the respective organizational risk appetite.

Regulatory guidance has long recognized the need for technology risk assessment as part of the new technology adoption cycle. OCC Bulletin 1998-3, issued all the way back in 1998, said it plainly:

> When considering whether to adopt a new technology or to upgrade existing systems, a bank should assess how it will use the technology within the context of its overall strategic goals and its market.[4]

The recognition of the inflow of new technology as a driver of risk has since been embedded in subsequent guidance. Many financial institutions have implemented this requirement via policy setting to ensure pre-implementation risk assessment is conducted prior to significant new technology deployments.

So what has changed since 1998? The pace of change, the complexity of financial systems, and the interconnection between institutions and markets, among other factors, have added to the urgency. The stakes are much higher as the consequences for risk events continue to grow. The potential for the introduction of vulnerabilities via new technologies continues to expand as well.

Human Vulnerability Dimensions

It is clear human factors have the potential to become, or create, vulnerabilities. The nature of the trusted insider role in all organizations necessarily brings us to one of the core challenges of cybersecurity: providing the "appropriate" level of access to the "correct" people at the "right" time. Practical complexities, such as the timing dimensions of the access granting process, cause some of the challenges, such as when an employee vetted through background checks may subsequently become a threat. Another possibility is the individual seeking access to systems and data is already very much a threat but simply has not yet been caught and therefore appears to be an acceptable system user. Staff not provided with security training that reflects current threats may unwittingly become vulnerable, as they may be unprepared for emerging attack patterns. It is reasons such as these that should cause cybersecurity leaders to temper the currently widespread assumptions of the effectiveness of background searches.

This is not to suggest background searches are unimportant. On the contrary, they are a crucial control to *reduce or prevent* insider cybersecurity risks. A challenge, however, is we see a very high level of reliance on background searches without complementary controls that could provide *detective* or *response* benefits that would treat dimensions such as the timing factors described earlier. Challenges associated with the human dimensions of cybersecurity should therefore be viewed *programmatically*, such that the controls design includes successive layering of individual risk treatments. For example, background searches can reduce or prevent, monitoring of privileged account usage can detect, and specialized steps for investigating insiders can guide the response.

Another important concept with respect to insiders is the consideration of both intentional and unintentional factors. Much attention has been provided to the scenario of the purposeful insider that undertakes deliberately hostile actions. Hostile insiders can act as a sort of "sleeper cell" within an enterprise, gaining access via legitimate means until such time as they are activated and begin leveraging their appropriately assigned access privileges to undertake harmful actions. Examples include the numerous cases of trusted bank employees who, sometimes after long periods of trustworthy employment, begin stealing customer data to facilitate identity theft. Triggers for a previously vetted insider to begin acting badly could potentially be financial gain but could also reflect the emotional reactions of disgruntled staff. Regardless of motive, the challenge remains that heavy emphasis on vetting without complementary detective and response controls after access has been granted is not a sound strategy.

Unintentional vulnerabilities generally evolve around a lack of knowledge or understanding on the part of the insider. Knowledge requirements change over time, thereby creating the need for continuous education and training. A staff member with weak understanding of their respective process and systems environments represents a prime target of attackers who have a range of technical and social engineering tactics at the ready to pounce on unprepared members of an organization.

Weak business process designs can similarly create vulnerabilities. Very often, internal audit and controls oversight focus on evaluation of the controls design and operating effectiveness of controls. However, greater problems may exist in the form of undetected vulnerabilities in processes. Segregation of duties (SOD), for example, is often built into the business process design as a fundamental control strategy. The reliance on SOD is commonplace within financial institutions. The American Institute of Cerfified Public Accountants (AICPA) describes the vulnerability of an environment without SOD as follows:

> Imagine what would happen if the keys, lock and code for a nuclear weapons system were all in the hands of one person! Emotions, coercion, blackmail, fraud, human error and disinformation could cause grave and expensive one-sided actions that can't be corrected. Or, consider the software engineer who has the authority to move code into production without oversight, quality assurance or access rights' authentication.[5]

SOD has been historically viewed, appropriately, as a vital controls strategy. However, it is obviously not effective in controlling against the risks of collusion–that is, the cooperation of multiple parties to ultimately result in unwanted actions, such as various types of financial frauds. The challenge is very real; collusion between trusted insiders can and does regularly occur. To ignore this, or simply follow traditional controls thinking such as "you can't control for collusion," is too simplistic in the current environment. This again illustrates the need for a layered environment of protective, detective, and response controls as suggested earlier. Additionally, fraud detection efforts ideally should be viewed as part of, or complementary to, the internal controls environment, as they represent a sort of tripwire to detect the negative events that may suggest the enterprise has been compromised.

An Illustration: Business E-mail Compromise

The growing frequency and severity of "Business E-mail Compromise" (BEC) is a vivid illustration of the cumulative effects of multiple forms of vulnerability. BEC is not a new phenomenon, nor is it significantly sophisticated from a technological perspective. It has proven, however, to be highly effective in separating large amounts of money from otherwise successful and well-managed organizations by leveraging a range of human vulnerabilities. Various sources place the losses in the billions of dollars, and the percentage of organizations targeted at almost 90 percent.[6] BEC is a threat that seeks to exploit people, process, and technology vulnerabilities within a single attack.

Although the attack specifics may vary, the FBI has identified the following common stages to a BEC attack[7]:

1. Identification of target: This may be accomplished through publicly available resources, including websites and annual reports.

2. Grooming of victim: The adversary uses a social engineering technique such as spear-phishing or pre-text telephone calls to persuade and potentially intimidate an employee, often someone with authority to complete banking and other financial transactions. This stage could take days, weeks, or months.

3. Exchange of information: Once the grooming has been deemed effective, the adversary will initiate what they characterize as a legitimate financial transaction, such as a request for the victim organization to direct funds to the adversary.

4. Wire transfer: Ultimately the adversary will convince the victim to electronically transfer funds into the adversary's primary account. Once the funds enter the adversary's primary account, the adversary will move the funds to a secondary account.

The complexity of the vulnerability landscape comes into view when considering the nature of the vulnerabilities exploited during a BEC. There are technical elements, such as the use of bogus, deceptive e-mail messages that included links to malicious code or may trigger delivery of malicious code upon the message being opened by the victim. There are obvious human dimensions as well: distracted or unprepared employees may unwittingly fall prey to BEC. Process dimensions are clear as well. Once the victim's e-mail account is compromised, the adversary may be able to quickly identify process control weaknesses, such as inadequate approval layers, and thus craft the deceptive approach to exploit process deficiencies. There are certainly potential risk treatments to reduce the vulnerabilities visible in the BEC scenario. The challenge, however, is deploying multiple, reliable controls that will actually be *consistently effective* in stopping a determined threat actor who understands common vulnerabilities very well and has nothing better to do than attempt to fool your staff to give away your money.

Understanding the Consequences

The term "breach" connotes a violation, as in a breach of trust, breach of faith, or breach of promise. In cybersecurity, breach also conveys another meaning that carries an even greater negative relevance for financial institutions-it may also indicate a gap. Taken literally, a breach or gap can only refer to one or more cybersecurity controls, where the term control in this context refers to management control over business operations. Moreover, the cybersecurity context refers specifically to technology controls, the subset of enterprise controls that enable management to control technology. Therefore, the potential for a cybersecurity breach is a major concern for any business that relies heavily on "preventive" technology controls to protect and preserve data. Cybersecurity controls are intended to prevent or reduce harm to the confidentiality, integrity, or availability of data. When these controls are broken, it means management does not fully control the technology it uses to provide financial operations.

Financial industry concern with cybersecurity breaches is justified mainly because of the potential for a variety of negative consequences. Even small breaches with minimal impact on the bottom line present a fundamental concern with the management culture that allowed them. A financial institution's business model is based on trust that management can maintain the integrity of financial transactions and protect and preserve financial assets. All financial assets are maintained on computer systems, and so a cybersecurity breach of any size presents immediate and significant reputational risk.

Although there are information security controls designed to detect when preventive controls fail, and/or recover from breaches in preventive cybersecurity controls, it is important to understand that detection and recovery mechanisms are not the primary controls that are violated in a cyberattack. For these detection and recovery controls to be utilized and provide value, a breach in preventive control has already occurred. Hence, a cyberattack that is not immediately detected and remediated is cause for even greater concern than one that is immediately remedied. It is also important to understand not all control breaches are the consequence of cyberattacks. A preventive control may be breached due to human error or negligence, and these same detection and recovery controls are expected to be effective. However, for the purpose of this discussion, we will adopt a narrow definition of cybersecurity breach that refers only to a situation in which information security preventive controls fail to protect the confidentiality, integrity, or availability of data from a malicious adversary. That is, we define a cybersecurity breach in a financial institution as a breakdown in management control over data.

As the US Federal Financial Institutions Examination Council has described, potential adverse effects of control weaknesses can arise from the following:[8]

- Disclosure of information to unauthorized individuals

- Unavailability or degradation of services

- Misappropriation or theft of information or services

- Modification or destruction of systems or information

- Records that are not timely, accurate, complete, or consistent

The impact will differ depending on attributes of the breach, ranging from whether it resulted in information loss (confidentiality control breach), account takeover fraud (integrity control breach), and/or interruption in financial services (availability control breach). Only in the third case, and only in particularly effective attacks, will the breach be guaranteed to become public knowledge. For this reason, many financial institutions are tempted to classify cybersecurity breach events as some other coincident event type related to the impact.

For example, a cybersecurity breach wherein consumer credit card data is stolen by intruders who then use it to create fraudulent charges may be classified as "Card not present" fraud, a generic term for using the phone or the internet to make a purchase so that the merchant cannot verify the cardholder is in possession of the card. This type of fraud can occur when people lose their wallets, so the category does not necessarily refer to the real root cause: the successful cyberattack. The customers who are impacted may suspect some lapse in confidentiality control, but this will not make headline news. Avoidance of reputational risk is an instinctive reaction in the financial industry, prompted by fear of a "run on the bank." Although the gut reaction is not always well–thought-through, the logic is that if a bank cannot maintain cybersecurity access controls, it may not be able to maintain other preventive controls such as balance integrity and account availability.

Note the definition of a cybersecurity breach in a financial institution, as a breakdown in management control over data does not necessarily imply the institution had appropriate controls in place and they were somehow bypassed. Planning for appropriate controls as part of business requirements for technology is itself a control objective for information technology. Table 2-1 shows how the Information Systems Audit and Control Association (ISACA) has recommended that risk considerations be integrated into the technology planning process.[10] The risk of a cybersecurity breach can be divided into the three commonly accepted control objectives that may be breached: confidentiality, integrity, and availability of information, but there are multiple dimensions of impact to financial services when these fundamental controls are breached, and

Table 2-1 shows how ubiquitous security considerations are in all aspects of technology management. It clearly demonstrates how well established cybersecurity risk considerations are in the professional practice of technology controls.

Table 2-1. *ISACA Processes Reference to Cybersecurity Risk*[9]

Process Domain	Cybersecurity-Related Control Principals
Evaluate, Direct, and Monitor	Ensure Risk Optimization
Align, Plan, and Organize	Manage Security
Build, Acquire, and Implement	Manage Requirements Definition Manage Change Manage Assets Manage Configuration
Deliver, Service, and Support	Manage Service Requests and Incidents Manage Continuity Manage Security Services
Monitor, Evaluate, and Assess	Monitor, Evaluate, and Assess the System of Internal Control

The message for financial institutions is there needs to be a cybersecurity control environment within the technology infrastructure, whether in-sourced or out-sourced, whether planned or simply emergent. If planned, the extent to which information confidentiality, integrity, and availability are protected from cyber threats is, if not known, at least knowable. The distinction between known and knowable is a matter of measuring attributes of the information technology control environment that was implemented based on the plan. However, if not planned, the extent to which information is protected is not actually knowable, and it is highly probable that information is extremely vulnerable. Cybersecurity controls are hard enough to maintain and monitor today when very smart people are paying close attention to the rapidly changing environment. Without close attention, perhaps due to the responsibility delegated to a central security group, then the risk is not necessarily that a control will be breached but that controls will be absent. In this situation, a professional assessment will sometimes phrase their conclusion that controls are "weak."

The best way to understand breach impact is to identify potential risk scenarios where cybersecurity controls may be stretched to their limit and to determine the consequences that would be the outcome of the scenario considered as the proximate cause. The word proximate is intended to check the temptation to leap from a cybersecurity event as a root cause to commonly assumed outcomes. For example, a malware attack considered as a root cause leads to assumptions of intermediate software process failures cascading into a situation where all desktops are unavailable. But considered as a proximate cause of a cybersecurity breach to a specific financial institution, general knowledge of malware attacks is not enough. Much more needs to be understood about the operation of a relevant sample of malware specimens to which an institution is vulnerable, its method of infiltrating the first internal machine on which it was loaded, and the potential downstream consequences of its install on the broader financial institution's environment.

Malware attacks are a great example due to the amount of detailed analysis they have undergone since the 1980s.[11] The Lockheed Martin Cyber Kill Chain, described earlier, can be used as the basis for malware scenario analysis by describing the common series of sequential steps executed by a determined adversary.[12]

Vulnerability Assessment via scenario analysis entails researching the steps in the attack, brainstorming with experts in the attack scenario (in this case, malware analysts), and coming up with as complete as possible set of plausible attack vectors. In a malware scenario, examples can focus on malicious software that is compatible with internal operating systems, adversaries that are known to be motivated to attack your financial institution or similar institutions, and information that is readily available to internal users. This is important because the financial industry has a long undeniable history of being exploited from the inside, and increasing incidents of pervasive espionage should be assumed to be possible in the context of any financial institution's scenario analysis exercises. In short, scenarios should assume all information available to internal users on the internal network is already in the hands of your adversary as a result of the reconnaissance step of the attack, along with internet port scans and harvesting of social media posts by employees, contractors, and customers.

In a malware scenario analysis, technical attack vectors to which an institution is vulnerable are presented in tabular format to determine if controls are in place to thwart each step of the attack. Table 2-2 is an example for an institution that has a three-tiered technology architecture with Microsoft desktops, Linux web server, and mainframe databases.

Table 2-2. *Example Malware Attack Vectors*

Kill Chain Step	Attack 1	Attack 2	*Controls*
Reconnaissance	Internet scan reveals web server internal IPs and software	Internet scan reveals e-mail remote access server version	None
Weaponization	Creates malware that scans internal networks for web server vulnerabilities	Creates malware that attaches itself to remote access e-mail client outbox	None
Delivery	Sends malware in link in e-mail to web server admins disguised as software update notice from web vendor	Sends fake shopping links via e-mail to home e-mail addresses of internal users known to use mainframe database	Partial Inbound spam and phishing e-mail filters
Exploitation	Admin clicks on link that starts downloads weapon.	Users click on link that downloads weapon.	Partial User education to avoid phishing e-mail Proxy sandboxes for admins

(continued)

Table 2-2. (*continued*)

Kill Chain Step	Attack 1	Attack 2	*Controls*
Installation	Browser scripts install malware on admin desktop as a background service	E-mail client is loaded with script that exploits internal e-mail client auto-execute capability to install itself on browser of internal remotely accessible desktop on send	Partial Desktop anti-virus Proxy sandboxes for admins
Command and Control	Adversary directs malware to run scan, find webservers, exploit web software vulnerabilities to find user data, and leave on web server for pickup by adversary	Every time browser starts up, it accesses adversary website to send data and retrieve next command. Over time, it identifies mainframe database, installs database client, retrieves data on behalf of user, and sends to file share site.	Minimal Sensitive data is restricted to secure file locations, and periodic scanning is in place to detect it in unauthorized locations.
Action on Objectives	Adversary retrieves data from webserver	Adversary retrieves data from file share site	Partial Known adversary sites are blocked, some file share sites are blocked.

Scenario analysis can be considered a type of "tabletop exercise" because it does not typically involve tests of exploits against systems, but instead relies on the system's subject matter experts to volunteer information about how their systems would respond to the scenario as presented. In this aspect, cybersecurity scenarios are very similar to a more traditional information security control self-assessments.[13] There are a few differences. One is that a more traditional information security self-assessment focuses on one system of interest. In cybersecurity scenario analysis, the focus is instead on just one specific type of threat to all systems in order to identify which systems may be vulnerable to that threat. Also, in traditional information security control self-assessment, the focus is purely on technology controls. In cybersecurity scenario analysis, all aspects of impact, reaction, and response may be considered, including potential public relations, legal, and human resources responses. Scenario analysis begins with scenario development, enlists a wide variety of expertise in the scenario selection process, and then follows up with select experts for joint discussion. This discussion is the "tabletop" and the attendees are tabletop participants. In the tabletop portion of a scenario analysis exercise, the invited participants review and comment on the scenario itself and then opine on how the controls in the current environment may or may not allow the institution to detect the adversary. In other words it illustrates the degree of post-control vulnerability. The questions that drive the scenario discussion are the same questions that these subject matter experts would be asked if there was a real security incident. Table 2-3 provides an example list of discussion points to facilitate the scenario analysis.

Table 2-3. *Discussion Points: Scenario Analysis[14]*

How would the problem initially be detected? When would it be detected and by whom?
What security infrastructure components exist in the affected environment? (e.g., firewall, anti-virus, etc.)
Which individuals would be aware of the incident? What are their names and group or company affiliations?
Who is authorized to make business decisions regarding the affected operations?
What mechanisms will the team to communicate when handling the incident?
Who is responsible for internal (or external) periodic progress updates and what schedule would they adopt?
Who would interface with legal, executive, public relations, and other relevant internal teams?
Which IT infrastructure components (servers, websites, networks, etc.) would be directly affected by the incident?
What applications and data processes make use of the affected IT infrastructure components?
Would there be compliance or legal obligations tied to the incident? Who is responsible for maintaining compliance?
What commands or tools would be executed on the affected systems?
What alerts would be generated by the existing security infrastructure components?
Are there specific incident response instructions or guidelines? What value would they add?
Who will be responsible for containing the incident to minimize its effect on neighboring IT resources and to eliminate compromised artifacts, if necessary, on the path to recovery?

In the course of discussion of these specific technology and operational aspects of the scenario, control weaknesses are identified and new controls may be designed to mitigate the known threats. The take-away from this discussion is that a financial institution's internal subject matter experts know how vulnerable the institution is to cyberattack, but they are unlikely to volunteer that information in the absence of a safe and prudent approach to revelation and mitigation. If control weaknesses are systematically exposed, then management can take appropriate steps to correct them. In the absence of mechanisms for systematic exposure, it is unlikely that the subject matter experts will study hacker behavior until an attack actually occurs.

Cybersecurity control weaknesses are not just a reflection on technology management but can be a root cause of transactional, strategic, reputational, and compliance risks. This crosses a wide range of managerial responsibility that spans financial product owners, risk managers, public relations, and corporate lawyers. Table 2-4 lists just a few damaging impacts to confidentiality, integrity, and availability that have occurred due to technology failures and could have a cybersecurity breach as a root cause.

Table 2-4. *Potential Impact of Cybersecurity Control Weaknesses*

Control Category	Potential Impact of Control Weaknesses
Confidentiality	• Customers being shown each other's data from the internet • Employees selling customer personally identifiable information to organized crime • Hackers changing account numbers in browsers to see data from other's accounts
Integrity	• Executed transactions missing from statements resulting in inaccurate customer balances • Incorrect employee withholding tax calculations • Help desks overwhelmed with calls from employees reporting errors in reports generated by business applications

(continued)

Table 2-4. (*continued*)

Control Category	Potential Impact of Control Weaknesses
Availability	• Brokers, customer service centers, and tellers without desktops cannot perform their job function • Systems developers unable to access the internet to download patches necessary to fix vulnerabilities • Countries cut off from global telecommunications services

Even one of the events listed in Table 2-4 could have a devastating impact on a financial institution, if made public, from a reputational risk perspective. Decades ago, such events were typically ignored by newspapers, as the root cause was typically human error, and the financial press considered bad taste to spread fear of the banking systems. But today, when events happen in financial institutions, there is always suspicion that it could be due to control weaknesses, and the cloak of press goodwill is no longer reliable. Regardless of the cause, when such events do happen, heroic technology engineers whose main job is not security often step in and save the day before reputational risk thresholds are noticeable to senior management. As more technology jobs are outsourced, these heroes will become fewer and further between. And as more cybersecurity jobs are disconnected from mainstream technology operations, the less these engineers will understand about the cybersecurity controls meant to protect and preserve their systems. Technology managers who have wishfully concluded that cybersecurity is not their job are often surprised to find that they are the ones expected to dig their company out of the consequences of a breach.

Moving Ahead

The potential impact from breaches of confidentiality, integrity, and availability as summarized in Table 2-4 can include a variety of disruptions and other negative effects. Expressing the impact to management requires quantification of impacts. This could include operational metrics such as service availability and response activities. Ideally such factors should be expressed in financial terms. The next chapter explores the challenges and potential approaches to illustrating how much a breach actually costs the organization.

Notes

1. Lockheed Martin Cyber Kill Chain. `https://www.lockheedmartin.com/en-us/capabilities/cyber/cyber-kill-chain.html`, 2018.

2. Apache.Org Statement on Struts Vulnerability Following Equifax 2017 Breach. `http://blogs.apache.org/foundation/entry/apache-struts-statement-on-equifax`

3. Moore, Geoffrey, *Crossing the Chasm*, 3rd Edition, (New York: Harper Business Publishing, 2014)..

4. Office of the Comptroller of the Currency (1998) OCC Bulletin 1998-3, `https://www.occ.gov/news-issuances/bulletins/1998/bulletin-1998-3.html`

5. AICPA (2018). Segregation of Duties.
    `https://www.aicpa.org/interestareas/`
    `informationtechnology/resources/auditing/`
    `internalcontrol/value-strategy-through-`
    `segregation-of-duties.html`

6. Muncaster, P. (2017) BEC Attacks Jumped 17%
    Last Year. *Infosecurity Magazine.* `https://www.`
    `infosecurity-magazine.com/news/bec-attacks-`
    `jumped-17-last-year/`

7. Federal Bureau of Investigation (2018) Business
    Email Compromise. `https://www.fbi.gov/news/`
    `stories/business-e-mail-compromise-on-the-`
    `rise`

8. Federal Financial Institutions Examination
    Council (FFIEC), FFIEC Information Technology
    Examination Handbook - Information Security
    Booklet, 2016.

9. EDP Auditors Association (EDPAA), Control
    Objectives (Handbook), EDPAA, 1977.

10. Information Systems Audit and Control Association
    (ISACA), COBIT5: Enabling Processes, 2012, see
    `www.isaca.org`.

11. For a walkthrough of the history, see Schmidt,
    Howard, *Patrolling Cyberspace*, (Blue Bell, PA:
    Larstan Publishing, 2006).

12.   Cloppert, Mike, (2009), `https://digital-forensics.sans.org/blog/2009/07/23/` , July 23, 2009, subsequently presented at Evolution of APT State of the ART and Intelligence-Driven Response. US Digital Forensic and Incident Response Summit `http://computer-forensics.sans.org`, 2010.

13.   Woody, Carol, "Applying OCTAVE: Practitioners Report," Software Engineering Institute Technical Note: CMU/SEI-2006-TN-010, Carnegie Mellon University, May 2006.

14.   These examples were adapted from `www.zeltser.com`, author Lenny Zeltser with thanks to Jack McCarthy and Patrick Nolan, in the document "Initial Security Incident Questionnaire for Responders," retrieved 1/6/2018.

CHAPTER 3

What Would a Breach Cost Us?

The impact, or consequences, of a cyber event can be substantial and complex. Costs can accrue as a result of disruptive effects on personnel, technical architecture, technology operations, business processes, customer impact, and regulatory exposure as well as a myriad of factors associated with the return to business as usual. Responses described in reporting on recent high-profile breaches have provided glimpses of varying organizational approaches to measuring actual impact. This has revealed high costs that stretch into areas well beyond the affected enterprise's preliminary consideration. Economic impact is difficult to measure, changes with respect to event characteristics and industry context, and can stretch over a significant period of time. Costs are very real and can be substantial.

Risk Quantification

Perhaps the most important aspect to consider when attempting calculating true costs of a breach is the importance of selecting an appropriate unit of measure. The selection does not depend on which currency defines a monetary unit; rather, it depends on what counts as a

© Paul Rohmeyer, Jennifer L. Bayuk 2019
P. Rohmeyer and J. L. Bayuk, *Financial Cybersecurity Risk Management*,
https://doi.org/10.1007/978-1-4842-4194-3_3

cost. Most operational risk management policies define losses as money spent that would not have been spent had the breach not occurred. This reduces the unit of measure to money leaving the organization. Even with these well-defined criteria, depending on how expenses are classified, an expense incurred by a breach may not be allowed to be included because the organization has allocated some amount of dollars toward an operating expense that is not dependent on any single event. For example, most financial institutions have a technology incident response capability with 24-7 operations. After a cybersecurity breach, technical staff may be totally consumed in incident response, recovery, and forensic activities.

For example, this is often the same staff responsible for continuous business operations. As they would be at work regardless, such individuals are viewed as a cost of doing business and not part of the marginal cost of any individual breach. For a more controversial example, consider that most financial institutions will purchase identity theft protection insurance for the customers impacted by a breach. In some institutions, the costs related to such customer identity theft protection are not considered operational losses caused by a breach but are instead classified in the general ledger as customer good will. These examples and others like them lead many who work in cybersecurity to claim that the true cost of a breach is typically underreported.

That is, it has been a constant source of surprise to cybersecurity professionals that financial institutions claim losses directly attributed to a cybersecurity breach are relatively small. That may be a reflection of the way banks sometimes may record operational losses as only direct expenses resulting from a breach. These are recorded only if an invoice is justified solely on the basis of recovering from a loss, such as transferring money into a customer's account or paying a vendor invoice to deliver hardware or software on an expedited basis.

Costs related to emergency configurations by existing employees are, by contrast, basic "run-the-bank" costs. This term is used in the industry to differentiate from "change-the-bank" costs. Run-the-bank costs include stable and predictable expenses such as real estate facilities, power, light, and office supplies that support current operations. Change-the-bank costs include projects with specific deliverables designed to enhance financial services or strengthen current operational controls. When staff whose jobs are required to run the bank have their skills diverted to recover from an emergency, that cost is still classified as operating expense. Moreover, even when staff dedicated to project work, such as software engineers, are diverted to investigate a cyber event, those expenses are absorbed by project overruns on the planned project. So, though not strictly run-the-bank costs, they are still not, in financial accounting, connected to the cybersecurity event.

Cybersecurity cost calculation typically does not consider that projects are delayed because the people who are working on a breach are not working on technology innovation. They do not consider loss of business from customers that move their accounts to another bank. These are opportunity costs, missed new business that may or may not have materialized—not money out the door. These units of measure are not likely to be directly attributed to a specific data breach (Figure 3-1).

Figure 3-1. *Breach impact analysis in practice*

The second most important aspect to understand about calculation of the cost of breaches is that any answer is at best an estimate. The cost of a breach will ultimately depend on business impact, a factor that is difficult to estimate until a breach actually occurs. Credit risk professionals have for decades collected historical data on past customer behavior in order to identify indicators that credit extended to a customer may not be paid back. Credit default consequences are calculated using the financial impact of transactions that have discreet numerical monetary value. Cybersecurity risk events are by nature highly variable, and the consequences are not limited to impacted transactions. Moreover, they may not even be calculated based on transactions impacted. There is often a time delay factor in the analysis of cybersecurity breach investigations when the set of transactions impacted is unknown or perhaps unknowable. Similarly, financial institutions routinely bear losses due to "card not present" credit card fraud, and it is often not possible to know whether a customer's authentication information was compromised via any given breach.

The fact is that business loss calculation is fixated on tangibles such as asset value and market value, while the cost of a cybersecurity breach is not directly correlated with the cost of the impacted computer assets or the cost of a cyber service such as a market data stream.[1] A cybersecurity event may cause an abrupt disruption of the operation of a system that cannot be fixed with the immediate replacement of the affected asset or service. Even if the physical asset or service were immediately available for replacement, it would have to be configured and integrated into a financial system for it to mitigate the impact of a breach. This response must be preplanned and, if it exists, is also charged to routine operating expense, and not considered part of the cost of any given breach.

A key to estimating what a theorized breach might cost is to analyze business systems that are dependent on technology in comparison with cyber risk events. A prerequisite to a systematic approach to determine breach impact is a business systems inventory. This allows a determination of how systems may be used to achieve the goals of a potential cyber attacker and allows a comprehensive list of possible cyber risk events to be constructed. With such a list, both individual and patterns of events can be analyzed in order to understand what actual change would befall people, processes, and technology and, from there, estimate the potential impact of that situation. This information should prompt the selection of units of measure for loss estimation and then a breach cost estimate may be determined, as illustrated in Figure 3-2.

Figure 3-2. *Estimated breach impact calculation*

Scenario Creation

Of course, not every possible technology misuse or disruption should be considered a potential cybersecurity event, and some taxonomical classification of risk that is unique to cybersecurity is appropriate. The Bank of International Settlements (BIS) Basel Committee guidance for sound operational risk directs banks to consider the full range of material operational risks when identifying both existing and potential to aggregate analysis of events that have similar root causes. It specifically refers to the following loss categories:[2]

- Internal fraud due to employee behavior

- External fraud due to unaffiliated criminals

- Employment practices and workplace safety

- Clients, products, and business practices

- Damage to physical assets

- Business disruption and system failures

- Execution, delivery, and process management, including unauthorized access and counterparty performance

Cybersecurity events may potentially be a root cause of risks in any of these loss categories, and scenario selection should consider all business processes which have the potential to result in substantial losses based on the types of event on this list. BIS guidance also directs banks to report on root-cause categories in aggregate.[3] This allows comparison of observed risk across business units and institutions for the purposes of capital allocation. ISACA's control processes, the Align, Plan and Organize Process: "Manage Risk" (APO012), recommends a list of generic scenarios be used to define a set of more relevant and customized scenarios, to enable a top-down view of the overall enterprise objectives and consider the most relevant and probable risk scenarios.[4]

Using the BIS categories as a tool in scenario selection has the benefit of providing completeness criteria to ensure that a wide variety of cybersecurity risk events are considered, at least at some high level. Cybersecurity losses, when recognized as such rather than being classified as fraud, had traditionally been embedded in more general, "business disruption and system failures" or "execution, delivery and process management" risk categories. This list was published in 2003, and regulators have since made it abundantly clear cybersecurity should be considered a top-tier risk. It is common for financial institutions to classify individual loss events in multiple categories for comparison across operational entities.

Note the word *scenario* in the context of operational risk is a term of art. Operational risk assessments typically define risk events at the category level, such as theft of funds due to wire transfer fraud. While these categories are helpful in understanding where the most serious impact may lie at a high level, until a hypothetical event is defined in detail, it will not be possible to identify exactly those systems impacted or to use data from affected systems to estimate losses. A practical approach to estimating the cost of any operational risk event, including a cybersecurity breach, is to use risk categories and business objectives to determine the most probable risk event categories that may impact the financial institution, then to define a realistic and probable scenario that can be used to drill down into each system to quantify potential impact. A scenario is a description of the activities leading up to, during, and after a risk event.

Figure 3-3 provides an example of a systematic approach to scenario creation. The universe of cybersecurity risk events is organized by the threat categories introduced in Chapter 1. Each goal is associated with two sets of variables: (1) technology that can be used to achieve the goal, and (2) access profiles that can achieve the goal using the technology. The adversaries are themselves then divided into communities with different access profiles. Note that there is no assumption in this simple breakdown that access is limited to authorized use, just an acknowledgement that different access profiles are associated with the technology environments that can be used to achieve an adversary goal. This information may be used to determine the situation that could result, which should be assessed as inherent risk, as it is the consequences of adversary goal achieved as if management control did not constrain goal achievement. This is not the same as assuming no controls are in place but recognition that somehow an adversary may be able to achieve the goal despite the controls that may be in place.

Adversary Objective	*Technology Scope*	*Adversary Access*	*Result*
Theft of Funds	Core Banking Systems	Internal	Loss of Deposits
Theft of Information	Mobile Banking	Internal	Data Exposure
Disruption	Corporate Systems	Breach of Privileged Account	Business Application Unavailable to Users

Figure 3-3. *Example approach to cybersecurity scenario creation*

Setting aside for a moment the question of whether an attack is probable given deployed controls allows the intellectual freedom to identify potential impact without explicitly critiquing the technology control operators upon whom a cybersecurity professional must rely to complete the analysis. That is, a simple assessment of potential consequences of adversary success serves to prioritize further analysis, as more scrutiny should be given to potential techniques by which a more damaging consequence may be achieved. Estimation of consequences given only system access in operation allows for prioritization of further scenario development work aimed at estimating financial impact and can be used to compare alternative scenarios in various stages of development.

Note that although our example is necessarily limited, in practice this analysis should be inclusive of all systems, and the technology scope should be narrowed only to the extent that systems provide value and access profiles in potential adversary communities differ. If an adversary changes profiles—that is, an attacker with third-party access gains internal access in the course of an attack—then the potential impact of that scenario would then be extended to include the impact accessible via the internal scenario. The same applies for internal users with end-user versus privileged access. The ability for an attacker to cross the line between access levels should itself be considered in the development of any scenario.

Figure 3-3 summarizes the impact of a successful attack, given the absence of preventive controls for a set of events that are in the general risk category "cybersecurity": "Theft of Funds," "Theft of Information," and "Disruption." The history of cybersecurity teaches us that any given control has some probability of not working due to technical or systemic vulnerabilities beyond the control of management, so each row in Figure 3-3 asserts there is some undetermined probability of an event in the cybersecurity risk category actually occurring. Leaving aside the actual estimation of probability for the moment, it is important to understand that Figure 3-3 suffices to explain that cybersecurity risk exists. Without consensus on this fact, it is difficult for stakeholders to take impact estimation seriously, and so must be settled among scenario development participants prior to moving on to the next step in figuring out what a breach might cost.

Scenario Selection

The next step is to move closer to realistic real-world cyber threat scenarios by comparing the theorized risk events to actual business processes susceptible operational loss categories (using guidance such as that issued by BIS) in order to credibly describe the business consequences. That is, we need to use knowledge of how actual systems work to create details of a scenario wherein the risk event occurs. As systems are composed of people, process, and technology, this knowledge includes, but is not limited to, adversary behavior patterns, software vulnerability patterns, current difficulties with technical control maintenance, and the actions or behavior of business users.

For example, the "Theft of Information" scenario in Figure 3-3 could be instantiated as a typical malware attack targeting end-user platforms via e-mail phishing or water cooler techniques that lure financial professionals with internet access to click on links that install software using their access levels (systems adversary behavior patterns), and search for common vulnerabilities that allow that software to escalate from end-user to administrative privileged access (software vulnerability patterns). A scenario customized for a specific organization would identify exactly which platform would be expected to have the vulnerability. It would identify the changes made to the platform by the malware (based on known technical maintenance issues) and from there identify the negative consequences for desktop software process and data impact. For example, software performance may degrade, and data may become inaccessible. The business would then be expected to call the help desk (business user behavior). This scenario description provides enough information for a team comprised of business, technical, and risk professionals to work out the details of impact.

Note this is just one potential risk event that could be used to tease out details in a systematic approach to deeper scenario creation. Simply, a scenario may be defined by four elements:

- Actor: a theoretical adversary with motivation, skills, resource

- Tactic: a technical workflow designed to achieve the adversary goal

- Target: a specific technology component that the actor must exploit to enact tactic

- Vulnerability: exposure in human actors, technology, or business process that enables tactic

In the earlier scenario, the critical elements are:

- Actor: Hacktivist

- Tactic: Phishing-deployed malware

- Target: Corporate Desktops

- Vulnerability: Operating System Security

To systematically analyze risk for all systems, these elements may be used to divide and conquer the overall risk analysis for exemplar events in each risk category that an organization may develop in the course of risk analysis. Of course, in conjunction with the observation that it is possible to divide and conquer such analysis, it is important to note that the potential values for each element may change over time and should always reflect current threat intelligence.

For example, a different set of actors, tactics, targets, and vulnerability can present an alternative scenario selection. Another potential scenario that may be derived from a description of disruption to corporate infrastructure using access of an internal end-user resulting in user productivity loss, business communication disruption, and desktop outages is the following:

- Actor: Nation state

- Target: Network routers

- Vulnerability: Heating, ventilation, and air conditioning (HVAC) vendor access network allows network routing commands to be introduced into corporate infrastructure

- Tactic: Infiltrate HVAC vendor, use maintenance connection to introduce default route that propagates and directs all network traffic to a domain owned by the nation state

Scenario creation based on this set of alternative elements suggests a situation wherein a well-funded professional crime organization targets HVAC devices, exploits vulnerabilities in HVAC vendor firewalls, and makes use of intelligence about internal corporate network vulnerabilities, perhaps from insiders. The actual scenario activities may be more debatable but must be considered plausible by all stakeholders, or, as previously noted, the lack of consensus may make it difficult for stakeholders to take impact estimation seriously. Note that it is especially hard for organizations that have considerable pride in strong controls to suspend their belief in those controls in order to facilitate cost analysis via the scenario. Individual scenarios that have low probability of occurrence may be eliminated as long as there is at least one scenario fully analyzed in each probable risk category.

Also note that although scenarios may be considered low probability due to strong controls, the opposite is also true. In the earlier example, a prevalence of dynamic routing architectures within the organization would increase the potential for a well-funded adversary to exploit known vulnerabilities in the internal network via the single vendor vulnerability posed by the scenario. In this way, the cost calculation from the scenario analysis may present a case for additional network routing controls to avoid losses.

Figure 3-4 provides alternative considerations for scenario development based on the four elements previously introduced in the earlier bulleted lists. Rather than threats to corporate infrastructure by end-users, we may consider threats to core banking systems by internal users. When an institution decides to calculate the cost of a potential breach, it is advisable to prepare such sets of potential alternatives in advance of the scenario selection(s). The plethora of examples serves to persuade doubters that at least one of the scenarios is possible, and discussion over which are more probable can start with some tangible ground truths that the team understands about the targeted environment. Note also that only one of the four alternative technical scenarios targets the core banking system itself. The focus on the financial assets rather than technical assets often leads to more creative speculation on potential for avenues for the adversary's technical attack.

Actor	*Target*	*Vulnerability*	*Tactic*
Hactivist	Microsoft Office Applications	Zero day desktop vulnerability	Macros on desktops of Core Banking System Users record application sessions and email back to hactivist site.
Organized Crime	BYOD Devices	BYOD sandbox loophole allowing unproxied web access	Malware on desktop controlled remotely (note transition from external to internal adversary), traversing network to find information from Core Banking Systems and stockpiling for bulk file transfer
Nation State	Core Banking System Database	Cloud Vendor firewall access flaw	Nation state infiltrates Cloud vendor with access to database queries into Core Banking System and bribes employee for admin connection string to be used from Cloud (note transition from third party to internal via loophole and insider collaboration)
Individual Fraudster	Network File Shares	Email content filter cannot read image files	Individual internal user uses authorized access to customer document scans on file shares, and emails it as attachment to external address to be used for identify theft

Figure 3-4. *Alternative cybersecurity scenario elements*

Cost Estimation

Much of the literature on the cost of cybersecurity breaches focuses on "theft of information" scenarios. Financial firms typically pay for credit report freezes and/or identity theft insurance for customers whose data was breached. They also incur legal costs of notifying customers that the breach occurred and these remedies are available. It is important for financial institutions to understand exactly what those mechanisms cost on a per-customer basis. These per-customer costs are routinely surveyed by multiple organizations; the most widely known is that performed by The Ponemon Institute.[5] The Ponemon Institute study relies on interviews with management in breached firms and attempts to quantify not only notification and legal costs, but also more hard-to-estimate variables as customer attrition and the efficacy of specific response activities in reducing the cost of a breach. They then divide the total cost of the breach by the number of records lost and compare those figures across industries, countries, and years. In the 2017 Ponemon study, the consolidated average per customer record was $141, the United States was the highest (at $225), and India was the lowest (at $64). The study did not claim to be a valid statistical exercise, so any individual company experience may differ. However, the data does provide some level of guidance.

In the absence of an actual, specific event to analyze, management must instead estimate the cost of a breach based on relevant experiences and reasoned analysis. Most cybersecurity scenarios are quantified on a sliding scale, estimating the expected duration of the event as the time it typically takes to identify and recover in the best and worst case. Current technology procedures may be used to determine the sequence of events that should be followed based on the first calls to the help desk and the expected activities of the technology operators, administrators, and engineers to whom the help desk escalates. It is typically the role of an independent risk or governance expert to walk through the procedures and historical data on events to make the determination of the expected scenario duration in a best or worst case of efficient and effective incident response and resolution. Information examined in such an exercise typically includes, but is not limited to, the following:

- Systems inventory of the full set of devices impacted by the breach

- Administration task history or business recovery test results showing how long administrators typically spend on system restoration tasks that would be required to recover from the cybersecurity attack

- The time it takes to reallocate technical resources in the escalation path who normally are assigned to other jobs, both consultants and employees such as developers, engineers, and architects

- The time it takes to onboard vendors who work on a time and materials basis

- The time it takes to install new equipment or software required to maintain systems availability

If procedures do not cover response to the type of incident under scrutiny, time must be allocated to capture the impact of uncertainty or confusion during initial response steps, as well as the eventual investigation. If there is no historical internal precedent, then industry data may be researched to the extent possible, using publications such as the annual Verizon Data Breach and Investigations Report.[6]

Even in cases where all response procedures seem to be in place, there may be uncertainty on variables such as staff or vendor availability or the time it may take a vendor to create a path for vulnerability. So, the impact quantification may be calculated for a half-day, full day, or 3 days. The walkthrough of procedures should ideally result in a list of activities that may be expected to occur throughout that time, such as the following:

- The Support/Help Center may quickly become overwhelmed as it devotes critical resources to work on nothing else for the duration of the incident.

- Cybersecurity teams spend that whole time in forensic analysis.

- Technology operations teams host incident response conference calls wherein engineers and executives to whom they have escalated spend time planning coordination of efforts (touching base every few hours).

- Application support teams perform emergency testing of desktop applications.

- Desktop administrators perform emergency patch installs.

- Cost of consultants or vendors to supplement workforce

- Cost of new equipment or software required to restore system availability

This represents a minimal description of technology expenses for illustration purposes only. All of these activities are consequences of the breach and could all be quantified as part of the breach cost. That is, it would be quantified as part of the breach cost if the cost of this labor were decided to count as a unit of measure in breach costs estimation. Assuming so, the costs for an organization are estimated in Figure 3-5.

	# Staff	Staff Level	Event Duration (hours)		
			6	24	60
1 Help Desk Special Task Force	2	Low	$600	$2,400	$6,000
2 Cybersecurity Forensics	2	Med	$900	$3,600	$9,000
3 Technology Incident Response					
Staff	2	Low	$600	$2,400	$6,000
Operations	2	Med	$900	$3,600	$9,000
Engineers	2	High	$1,500	$6,000	$15,000
Executives	2	Exec	$2,400	$9,600	$24,000
4 Application Support	2	Med	$900	$3,600	$9,000
5 Desktop Adminstrators	4	Low	$1,200	$4,800	$12,000
6 Cost of consultants and vendors	2	Exec	$2,400	$9,600	$24,000
7 Cost of new equipment of software			$50,000	$50,000	$50,000
Total Cost of Technology Activity:			$61,400	$95,600	$164,000
Cost for a large organization (multiply by 10):			$614,000	$956,000	$1,640,000

Figure 3-5. *Initial breach cost estimate: technology activities*

Figure 3-5 first calculates cost assuming the smallest possible organization that has requirements for 24-7 service levels. Because of vacations and other time off, full coverage of a single job in three shifts generally requires a technology company to ensure that there are six to eight people on staff that can perform the respective function. Of those, the figure assumes two individuals will be fully dedicated to the cybersecurity breach for the length of its duration. We assumed fully loaded hourly costs for staffing at $50 for staff positions, $75 for more highly skilled technologists, $125 for engineers, and $200 for executives. This hypothetical analysis also assumes typical management and consultant involvement in small business activities. Organizational size will also influence the relevant rates and other assumptions.

During the time of an incident, the business itself may be impacted as well. Where companies maintain a configuration management database that links technology devices to business applications, such an inventory can be used to list the users of business applications, which in turn may be useful to identify potential business process implications. In very large companies, users are sometimes surveyed to determine impact. However, it may also be possible that the business maintains measurements and metrics of business application throughput, and this combined with the estimated length of the breach may be used to estimate the costs of the cybersecurity breach in business terms. Note that many businesses have daily changes in business process throughout, so assumptions about time of day are typically important to define as well.

In our example, we will assume the equity sales brokers are without desktops and therefore cannot perform their job function. The result is productivity lost and also potential business lost. For business loss example, let us suppose the disruption would result in the inability to process customer equity buy and sell instructions and that this can be quantified in terms of transactions, and transactions as a unit of impact can be used to estimate the loss of commission revenue due to the breach.

Either or both of the productivity losses could count as a unit of measure in breach cost estimation, in terms of dollars spent on idle labor and the revenue loss in terms of lost commission. As in the case of technology, the business impact of the particular scenario would be quantified on a sliding scale. Using the expected duration of the event and historical data on customer use of the platform allows for calculation of the number of customer transactions impacted. The business impact of the unfulfilled transactions is quantified in terms of revenue lost and potential liability incurred for not executing orders already accepted. If the unit of measure includes opportunity cost, both numbers are included in the cost of the breach. If the unit of measure is simply money out the door, only the latter is counted.

Figure 3-5 shows an example of how the business transaction volume is distributed throughout a 24-hour time period. In the early morning hours, volume is only about 200 transactions per hour. The average peaks between 8 a.m. and noon, then subsides again, reaching its lowest per-hour volume at the end of the day. Although the sliding scale of the duration was chosen as 6, 24, and 60 hours, fees for the 8 a.m. to 8 p.m. 12-hour period appear in the figure to show how the 60-hour event is a multiple of two 24-hour periods plus one 12-hour period. Our analysis assumes a flat $10 per transaction commission and the opportunity cost as a direct multiple of the transactions that would be lost in each transaction volume distribution window.

In Figure 3-6, transaction count is also assumed to be the basis for calculating potential liability incurred for not executing orders already accepted. Let us assume orders received between 8 p.m. and 8 a.m. are not immediately processed but agreed upon by contract to be processed upon market open the next day. In the transaction metrics of Figure 3-6, the result is approximately 300 overnight transactions are potential liabilities, as they will not be processed in the morning but only after recovery from the event. In some of those 300 transactions, the market may be in the firm's favor, and the customer for whom the transaction is processed late will benefit financially from the delay, but in other cases, a loss may have occurred.

Hourly Equity Sales Metrics:				Event Duration (hours)		
12am-8am	8am-12pm	12pm-8pm	8pm-12pm	6	24	60
Time of event: 200	800	500	100	*transaction fee opportunity cost*		
8am-2pm: 0	3200	1000	0	$42,000		
8am-8am: 1600	3200	4000	400		$92,000	
Day1.8am-Day3.8pm: 3200	9600	12000	800			$256,000
Business Productivity Lost (5 staff @$150/hour):				$4,500	$18,000	$45,000
Business Transaction Fee Waived (night before):				$20,000	$20,000	$20,000
Business Transaction Goodwill Cost:				$7,500	$15,000	$22,500
Business Transaction Liabiity Cost:				$75,000	$150,000	$225,000
Total Business Transaction Cost:				$149,000	$295,000	$568,500

Figure 3-6. *Breach cost estimate: business transaction cost*

Figure 3-6 assumes that all of the overnight transactions will have their respective fees waived, representing an opportunity cost. Depending on the customer impact, the business may also decide to make the customer whole. It is further possible despite the fee waivers and goodwill gestures; a customer may sue for breach of agreement. In the goodwill case, the loss may be written off to "customer goodwill," a financial expense category that is not likely to appear in a breach loss calculation unit of measure. In the lawsuit case, any cost incurred will appear as a legal settlement, and this most certainly should be included in the cost of the breach.

Figure 3-6 assumes the firm will expend an average of $100 per transaction in goodwill for 25 percent of the overnight transactions, and the firm will settle for an average of $1,000 per transaction in liability fees for 5 percent of the transactions that are delayed in the 6-hour event. These amounts would differ for each duration category because the longer a transaction was delayed, the more likely customers would seek reimbursement. The 24-hour and 60-hour goodwill and liability costs are assumed to be double and triple the $100 and $1000 estimates, respectively.

As the scenario analysis team enumerates activities and events that incur costs, it will become apparent that opportunity costs other than lost business alone are being incurred, the opportunity costs of work not done. For example:

1. Administration task history will show how long administrators typically spend on routine tasks that are not performed during the cybersecurity response activity.

2. Project work on the application support side will be delayed, reducing time to market due to unavailability of application support teams.

3. User deliveries of desktop outputs will be delayed, such as management, client, and regulatory presentation materials.

These are typically not included as breach units of measure, but if they were, they would further increase the amount of the breach cost. The total cost of the breach would add these amounts to the amounts calculated in Figures 3-5 and 3-6. A quantitative valuation of lost income due to an assumption that a major market opportunity was missed or perhaps triggered regulatory fines resulting from the delayed work would also of course be relevant to management. In our example, we assume that such product delivery setback and fines cost $50K, $100K, and $200K for the 6-hour, 24-hour, and 60-hour events, respectively. This final assumption results in a full cost of cybersecurity breach estimate like the one illustrated in Figure 3-7. As in Figure 3-5, large organizations are represented as a multiple of 10.

Technology Activity Cost	$61,400	$95,600	$164,000
Total Business Transaction Cost	$149,000	$295,000	$568,500
Tech Admin Opportunity Cost	$50,000	$100,000	$200,000
Project Work Opportunity Cost	$50,000	$100,000	$200,000
End User Delivery Opportunity Cost	$50,000	$100,000	$200,000
Total Breach Cost Estimate	$360,400	$690,600	$1,332,500
Cost for a Large Organization	$3,604,000	$6,906,000	$13,325,000

Figure 3-7. *Total breach cost estimate*

Moving Ahead

In this chapter we have presented principles and approaches toward the efficient and pragmatic capture of relevant components of cyber breach costs. The considerations summarized here may be applied during after-action analyses, or as inputs in the forecasting of potential breaches. In the next chapter we will add another vital dimension to the forecasting challenge—the consideration of probabilities as we incorporate the potential likelihood of occurrence of theorized cyber incidents.

Notes

1. Borg, Scott, "The Economics of Loss," in *Enterprise Information Security & Privacy*, Axelrod, Bayuk & Schutzer, Eds., (Norwood, MA: Artech House, 2009).

2. Basel Committee on Banking Supervision (2003), Sound Practices for the Management and Supervision of Operational Risk (BCBS96, see: www.bis.org).

3. Basel Committee on Banking Supervision (2013) Principles for Effective Risk Data Aggregation and Risk Reporting (BCBS239 , see: `www.bis.org`).

4. ISACA (2012). COBIT5, Enabling Processes. Information Systems Audit and Control Association (`www.isaca.org`).

5. Ponemon Institute (2017). Cost of a Data Breach Study, Global Overview. `https://www.ibm.com/account/reg/us-en/signup?formid=urx-33316`

6. Verizon Enterprise. (2017). "2017 Data Breach Investigations Report, 10th Edition." `https://www.verizondigitalmedia.com/blog/2017/07/2017-verizon-data-breach-investigations-report/`

CHAPTER 4

What Are the Odds?

Financial industry standards, and corresponding regulations, thoroughly address the concepts of cybersecurity threat, vulnerability, consequences, and costs. Aspects of the threat landscape are communicated by organizations such as the FS-ISAC and through various public sector warnings and briefings. Vulnerabilities are both systemic and individual and becoming more widespread as technology evolves, and there is mounting evidence that withstanding or recovering from a cyber attack can be extremely expensive. Yet for many executives, a core question remains: what are the odds a cybersecurity attack will impact my institution? The question may at first seem suspect, given the large and growing array of relevant financial industry guidance on cyber. It would seem that any risk so obviously deemed critical by multiple overseeing bodies must of course have tangible impact on all financial institutions, but financial industry management has reason to think otherwise. That is, given all the standards and guidance on cybersecurity available to financial institutions, should we not be ahead of the curve?

Plausible Deniability

Rather than serve as a valuable warning bell, efforts to comply with cybersecurity guidance seem to have resulted, in some respects, in a misguided opinion among financial executives that compliance somehow suggests, if not "proves," their security measures are adequate.

© Paul Rohmeyer, Jennifer L. Bayuk 2019
P. Rohmeyer and J. L. Bayuk, *Financial Cybersecurity Risk Management*,
https://doi.org/10.1007/978-1-4842-4194-3_4

After the massive breach at Heartland, one of the largest financial services payment processors, the CEO launched what amounted to public relations campaign wherein the key message was, "Why didn't anyone tell me?"[1] According to reports, it had been the CEO's impression that compliance with standards and regulations adequately addressed the risks, and so he concluded his own firm's adherence to guidance indicated preparedness. Obviously, none of the apparent assumptions proved correct. The existence of standards and regulations, combined with the potential ramifications of admitting inadequate adherence, has created something of a culture of silence among cybersecurity professionals, as they may simply choose (perhaps for reasons of career self-preservation) to avoid directly challenging the views of their management.

This false sense of security is especially prevalent among organizational leaders who have taken expensive steps to install a qualified team of professionals charged with implementation of guidance and periodically subjected to outside audit, assessment, and examination. When successful attacks occur despite these efforts and investment, we sometimes hear comments about probabilities and the likelihood of cyber incidents that can occur despite deployed controls. The Heartland case in 2009 and the more recent Equifax case are such examples. In the case of Equifax, the company's executives did not attempt to directly defend themselves to charges of unpreparedness, although some pundits still did on their behalf.

That is, where cybersecurity programs are well-funded and led by responsible professionals, there sometimes seems to be a management assumption, or even declaration, that "cybersecurity risk" has been adequately addressed through compliance. However, there is little agreement in the risk management community on how exactly to define "cybersecurity risk" and less on how best to measure it. This therefore produces continuous uncertainty as to the appropriate design of controls. The result is an inflated prioritization of standards and guidance that by their nature reflect generalizations and cannot directly reflect risk considerations within specific, unique, enterprises. This mistake may occur despite appreciation throughout the industry that risks unique to the enterprise commonly present the most significant challenges.

A crucial aspect in examining cyber risk is the need to acknowledge that risks levels will never be reduced to zero in real-world environments. And so, despite regulations, standards, compliance, examiners, engineers, auditors, testers, and various other oversight professionals, there always remains a real chance of a negative outcome. We may build elegant theories and necessarily complex calculations to attempt to model risk; however, even the best models fall short of reality. In a constantly evolving threat environment we routinely see our risk models, and control decisions, become irrelevant due to ongoing vulnerability discovery and the continuous improvement of the adversary. In other words, we can fully comply with the best prevailing guidance, practices, standards, and regulations and yet STILL be victimized by a cyber breach. It is therefore productive to view cyber risk as it relates to the ongoing evolution of threats against business operations.

Cybersecurity Risk As Operational Risk

Although financial industry business executives commonly express surprise upon discovery of a breach, the success of cyber intrusions does not tend to shock technology risk managers. The constructs of risk management, as generally accepted by business today, has existed in more or less the same form for centuries. However, cybersecurity risk represents a problem space that has only in the past decade or so been examined in consideration of common operational risk criteria. In 1996, the history of risk management was chronicled in docu-dramatic form in a book by Peter Bernstein called *Against the Gods, The*

Remarkable Story of Risk.[2] Cybersecurity risk is not mentioned in the book, and none of the tools now used by cybersecurity risk managers existed. Bernstein was aware of the data analytics methods now used to analyze cybersecurity risk and referred to them as "computer gymnastics."

In Bernstein's view, the first mathematicians who thought about luck could easily have formed the body of knowledge that constitutes probability theory, but the idea of using math for risk management emerged only after people started to believe their own decisions could predict the course of providence, or fate. So while banks have been using credit models such as estimation of collateral and business rates of return for centuries, real mathematical models based on historical statistics were not used to guide business decisions until the Enlightenment, and by the seventeenth century the practice of combining historical data with statistics had become common in the insurance industry. Even today, the most clear-cut examples of financial executive risk decision-making are found in insurance, followed by credit. Whether credit is extended to a consumer, business, or government entity, some financial manager must estimate the odds the balance will be repaid. In the case of consumer credit risk, consumers are evaluated using a wide variety of dimensions, most significantly using credit scores that are risk indicators. Although the FICO[3] score is the most widely used measure, there are countless other scores based on models that include, but are not limited to, consumer demographics, income, currently extended credit, prior debtor experience, bankruptcies, court judgments, and liens.[4] Credit risk indicators serve as a proxy for a probability measure that the risk will not be repaid. Each bank will use such scores in some model that produces a measure of probability of whether a given consumer will pay off a given credit balance. The models are primarily based on past behavior of similar consumers in similar demographics and financial positions.

Another example of a domain where financial executives typically face risk-based decisions is market risk. Launching a new financial product or moving into a new financial market can be fraught with uncertainty. Executives conduct research wherein potential customers are surveyed to determine the probability that people will pay for the new product. Advertising strategies are analyzed to estimate the probability of reaching people who indicated interest in similar products, or are otherwise considered likely to be customers. Quotes are solicited from suppliers to estimate the probability that the product can be profitably produced. Armed with such probabilities, executives estimate the odds that a product launch will be successful and base decisions on those odds.

In all of the successful cases of the application of probability theory to risk management, there has been a large quantity of suitable data collected over time wherein stable patterns are repeated. Note that the credit risk decision is mostly based on analysis of historical data, and the market risk decision is mostly based on analysis of potential future behavior. Risk-based models of cybersecurity that use aggregated data sets to forecast the future are not yet commonly used by the industry. Without models that use past data to predict the future, there is no way to agree on a base probability of a given event. As Bernstein puts it, "forecasting tools based on nonlinear methods or on computer gymnastics are subject to many of the same hurdles that stand in the way of conventional probability theory: the raw material of the model is the data of the past."[5]

Credit risk decision parameters have been refined over the decades since the dawn of the information age. Although market risk decision models are not as standardized, the parameters that make up market risk decision models have also been researched and refined over decades. Data elements of use in predicting on cybersecurity events, however, have yet to be standardized in any manner that allows consensus on cybersecurity risk indicators. Furthermore there do not appear to be standards communities seeking ways to structure cybersecurity data so that future events may be forecast using data on past events. Although there has been some regulatory pressure on the financial industry to investigate such an approach, there is currently no equivalent of a credit score for cybersecurity. That is, standard risk management practices are of little use in reliably assigning relative probabilities of a successful cyberattack on two different systems or customers in the same way a banker can assign relative probabilities of successful mortgage payoff.

Shortage of Sufficient Historical Data

Newcomers to the field of cybersecurity may be surprised by the stark contrast between the ubiquity of headlines announcing cybersecurity attacks and the actual data available to study cybersecurity risk. This situation is certainly not the result of a lack of effort on the part of cybersecurity professionals to collect and share data. Indeed, from the first National Institute of Standards and Technology (NIST) conference on security metrics,[6] to the most recently formed institution, the Financial Systemic Analysis & Resilience Center (FSARC)[7], there have been heroic efforts to collect more, and better, data to support cybersecurity risk analysis.

The most notable efforts in between have been the Data Loss DB[8] and the Vocabulary for Event Recording and Incident Sharing (VERIS) Data Breach report.[9] Both have provided details on cybersecurity incidents but have struggled with the challenge of collecting a level of detail necessary to have utility from a statistical perspective. The VERIS report, also known as the Verizon Data Breach Investigations Report (DBIR), is the most data-rich, and includes case information from numerous sources including public and private incident response teams, international law enforcement agencies, cybersecurity software and services vendors, and think tanks.

Nevertheless, the data we have does not include enough relevant and meaningful detail to enable forecasting. Data collected on incidents is classified in a comparative taxonomy, verified to have occurred within a time frame of analysis, and attributable to an organization known to have similar characteristics. However it is not representative of the sizable range of cyberattacks that exist. The DataLoss DB disbanded as subscription services were anticipated, but none became predominant. As the VERIS report admitted in its most recent publication, "We have no way of knowing what proportion of all data breaches are represented because we have no way of knowing the total number of data breaches across all organizations in 2016. Many breaches go unreported (though our sample does contain many of those). Many more are as yet unknown by the victim."[10] Moreover, unless the attack is so widespread it hits thousands of machines at once, such as WannaCry,[11] incident data shared in bulk does not provide sufficient granular, technical detail to enable the comparison of two attacks and confirm they are, in fact, duplicate instances of the same attack.

Unfortunately, cybersecurity is a "wicked" problem, where wicked refers to the nature of a problem for which there is no ultimate, correct, solution but merely a goal of situational improvement for which the planner has solemn accountability.[12] The term "wicked" applied to "problem" was coined by sociologists searching for adjectives to describe their view of problems like homelessness and drug abuse. Systems security measurement shares an "inability to be totally solved" attribute common to those social science challenges and thus presents a problem of wicked proportion.

This makes it difficult to arrive at a concept of security that will allow it to be understood as a tangible systems attribute and to validate its measurement according to scientific standards. As Dan Geer, a founding member of securitymetrics.org, put it: "Speaking as a once-upon-a-time statistician, one has to ask if we are at the hypothesis testing stage or still at the hypothesis generation stage. I know that I am at the latter which is more or less why I am always looking for data on which I can do some exploratory analysis. People who have data can do hypothesis testing, of course, but as with the rest of science, once someone has generated and tested an hypothesis, then reporting it with sufficient attention to the 'Methods' section is so important-others can then do the verification step with their own data/apparatus/analysis."[13]

However unusable probability measures may be without data, there is absolute certainly that all systems connected to the internet are continuously scanned by malicious forces that use automated and manual techniques. There is an extremely high probability vulnerabilities will be found and exploited on any internet-connected system. The unknown is whether a specific adversary will target any given system. Over the past decade, there has been some data collected on targets. This changes from year to year, but affiliation with the financial industry has typically been a data point collected. One of the most data-rich studies on security breaches is the annual Verizon Data Breach Investigations Report (DBIR) that includes case information from numerous sources including public and private incident response teams, international law enforcement agencies, cybersecurity software and services vendors, and think tanks. According to the DBIR, in 2016 the Financial Industry experienced 24 percent of the reported cybersecurity data breaches, with healthcare coming in second at 15 percent, government third at 12 percent, and all 18 other industries sharing the remaining 49 percent. The report further shows that the financial industry also experienced 24 percent of the total number of reported incidents, although only ~1 percent of recorded incidents resulted in an actual data breach. So although every institution must estimate threat probability based on their own situational awareness, the best data available shows that for any given attack there is about a 1 in 4 chance that the target is a financial institution.

To be clear, it is not an overstatement to claim adversaries will scan all internet-connected systems registered to all financial services companies, and that it is plainly negligent for any financial services executive to assume that the probability that their firm is scanned for any new or old vulnerability is significantly less than 100 percent. It should also be clear that adversaries could exploit any vulnerable system. It follows that the probability a vulnerable financial system will be exploited is based not on whether it is a scanning target but on whether an adversary (who finds the vulnerable system in a scan) decides to exploit the vulnerability in pursuit of a goal of information theft, fraud, or disruption. That is, the measure of risk of exploit must be based on the attractiveness of a system as a target to a specific adversary. So the odds of being attacked can be concluded to represent the odds a system had vulnerabilities in combination with the odds that a skilled attacker will target them.

If these probabilities were independent, there would be a reduction in overall probability of being attacked due to uncertainty of the decision of the attacker. In a world where the probability of a system being vulnerable and the probability of it being exploited are 75 percent and 75 percent, respectively, the probability of the intersection can be illustrated as follows:

$$P(cyberattack_S) = P(vulnerability_S) * P(exploit_S)$$

$$= 0.75 * 0.75$$

$$= 0.5625 = 56.25\%$$

This explains why, despite the fact executives know the probability of vulnerabilities are high, they nonetheless often seem to believe their odds of being attacked are more like 50-50, or the luck of the draw (Figure 4-1).

However, the fact cybercriminals can be counted on to attack vulnerable banks means these probabilities are not actually independent. Rather, the set of situations in which there will be a cyberattack is the intersection of the set of systems in which there are vulnerabilities *is* the set of the systems in which an attacker chooses to exploit vulnerability. In this case, the probability of the intersection looks like this:

$$P(cyberattack_S) = P(vulnerability_S) * P(exploit_S|vulnerable_S)$$

$$= 0.75 * 1$$

$$= 0.75 = 75\%$$

Figure 4-1. *Estimating the odds*

Probabilities Driven by Vulnerabilities

The message here is clear: part of the answer is to reduce vulnerabilities. All financial institutions are attractive as a target to at least one prototypical adversary: organized crime. Sophisticated cybercrime organizations have been observed for over a decade,[15] and their activities feed a well-oiled machine of selling Personally Identifiable Information (PII) to facilitate frauds and identity theft cases.[16] Financial services companies, especially those with any name recognition, must acknowledge successful past attacks are likely to continue and be wary of the reality a number of as yet unidentified and unexploited vulnerabilities remain to be targeted.

In other words, once a newly identified vulnerability is published, and if the vulnerability is severe and easily identified via a scan, all websites recognizable as financial institutions will be systematically scanned by organized crime, and all financial institutions have a 100 percent probability of being attacked for this reason. In other words, a successful breach establishes an attractive pattern for inevitable "copy cat" attacks.

The first stage in any cyberattack is precisely this type of reconnaissance, and the 2017 Apache Struts vulnerability is a good example. At the time the vulnerability was announced, there were a high number of vulnerable financial institutions that a criminal could target and move from reconnaissance to more intrusive attack methods almost immediately. After the vulnerability was announced, many financial institutions directed web analytics teams to see if there was evidence in their Apache logs that attackers had exploited the vulnerability. At the time, several financial institutions immediately noticed the reconnaissance activity and immediately patched the vulnerability. It is likely that the adversary who targeted Equifax did so because it did not patch the Apache Struts vulnerability, and the failure to patch was directly observable. The known severity of the vulnerability may have provided a motive for in-depth reconnaissance, and the intruders identified additional vulnerabilities that were used in combination to achieve the threat objective: "Theft of Information."[17] It remains a mystery to readers of various public reports of the attack why Equifax did not seem to understand the odds were so strongly against them.

One reason could perhaps be the trust standards for the financial industry that includes demonstrated ability to withstand simulated attacks. For many financial institutions, the primary method of estimating the odds of adversary success is to mimic the full life cycle of an attack and count the pseudo-attacker success rate. Many financial companies employ independent consultants to pose as cyber attackers ("white hats") and try to achieve information theft or fraud, without being detected. This notably includes "penetration test" services ("pen tests" for short). The rationale for relying on pen tests is twofold: (1) it is assumed if pen testers achieve access to an application or defense layer, their efforts to access others are a good indication of the probability an attacker could figure out how to do so, and (2) it is assumed all known vulnerabilities will be scanned by the pen test team, so a pen test will demonstrate effective controls against all currently known vulnerabilities. Both of these assumptions are problematic, for different reasons. First, the skill levels of pen test teams are inherently variable, the scanning methods may widely differ; and second, the commercial teams are not nearly as well-resourced as sophisticated adversaries such as nation-states or organized crime.

However, the rationale of calculating odds of being attacked based on attacker ability to achieve objectives does make sense. Attacker objectives may be thwarted in two ways. One is to react quickly to mitigate known severe vulnerabilities, and the other is to not rely on any single control to prevent an attacker from achieving an objective. A system wherein an attacker objective can be achieved by exploiting a single vulnerability is well-understood to be fragile, and the odds of successful attack are reduced if more than one control would have to be vulnerable for an attacker to achieve an objective. The catchphrase "defense-in-depth" was coined for just this reason. The architecture underlying many financial institution defense-in-depth models implies that an attacker goal cannot be achieved unless at least once control at each layer of a multi-level infrastructure is broken. This is a "the chain is only as strong as its weakest link" view of vulnerability. As such, it relies on the strength of every layer to increase the odds that attacks are thwarted.

Figures 4-2 and 4-3 illustrate how the term defense-in-depth is commonly used but also, like pen tests, why it can sometimes be misleading. The concentric circles in the diagram evoke an image of barriers in the way of an intruder who attempted to move from one layer of technology infrastructure to the next. The smaller filled circles represent an authentication challenge and the bridges represent the ability for a user to bypass challenge at a defense-in-depth layer in order to proceed directly to a layer beneath it. It is not uncommon for a CISO to refer to a diagram such as that of Figure 4-2 when describing infrastructure level controls in a financial systems technology environment. The figure shows that each type of infrastructure is configured to require authentication. However, viewed holistically, the architecture of the infrastructure does not substantiate a claim of true defense-in-depth.

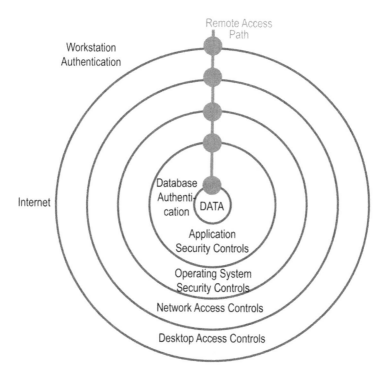

Figure 4-2. *Infrastructure level controls*

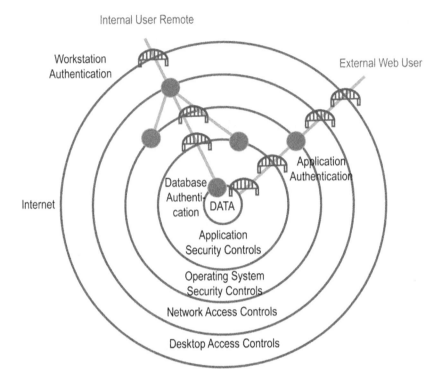

Figure 4-3. *Access paths*

Although the concentric circles in a defense-in-depth diagram evoke an image of strict segregation, in many financial services networks, the inner circle authentication mechanisms are *all* available on the *same* network (referred to as a "flat" network). So once a user is connected to the network (the outer-most layer), no firewall or other network control prevents the user from attempting direct authentication to other platforms and/or scanning for vulnerabilities on other platforms within the network. Where application users are expected to require access to multiple defense-in-depth layers, the infrastructure is also typically engineered to allow authenticated users in one infrastructure component to send commands to other components via automated "pass-through" mechanisms, commonly known as software services or microservices. Figure 4-3 traces the places where internal and external users following an access path are typically challenged for authentication before accessing resources.

The "Internal User Remote Access Path" in Figure 4-3 shows that, although there are two layers that require authentication between the network layer and the database layer, the database login prompt is available directly from the network via a port on the operating system where the database is installed. The figure demonstrates that when internal users log in remotely, they have only to authenticate to the network in order to reach the database front door directly. Many desktop tools, such as Microsoft Excel, provide mechanisms to authenticate directly to database ports that do not require operating system or application authentication.

The "External Web User Path" in Figure 4-3 demonstrates that when internet application users, such as customers, access the network, they authenticate at only one layer in the infrastructure: the application layer. After web users log in to an application, they do not need to provide further authentication for their data requests to be passed onto a database server. The application itself typically has access rights to the database server and sends queries to it on behalf of the user via a software service. These service-oriented architecture, or microservices, mechanisms are created for the sole reason that they allow application users to bypass a login prompt at the database layer.

Figure 4-3 therefore shows that highly confidential customer data is not concealed behind five layers at all times, because access to it only requires one authentication. The initial attack in the 2014 JPMorgan Chase data breach exploited a weak control on the network layer, a configuration similar to the internal user remote access path in Figure 4-3.[18] In the JPMorgan Chase hack, weak controls in some internal authentication mechanisms allowed the attacker to move through the internal network. The breached Equifax web application was configured in a manner similar to the Web User path in Figure 4-3. But the Apache Struts vulnerability allowed the attackers to bypass that single point of authentication, a situation wherein no access controls were required from the internet. Although the financial industry standard defense-in-depth architecture looks like Figure 4-2, every firm will have their own engineers configure authorized shortcuts as in Figure 4-3.

The recognition that customer data is often separated from attackers by a single password prompted the Federal Deposit Insurance Corporation in 2004 to issue a paper entitled, "Putting an End to Account-Hijacking Identity Theft." In it, they established guidelines for financial institutions to require customers to use a second authentication "factor," to be considered in authentication protocols, in addition to the traditional password method of granting access. At the time, there was one mechanism commonly referred to as the second authentication factor: a hand-held token. The mantra among security professionals with respect to factors at the time was:[19]

1.   What you know (password or passphrase)

2.   What you have (hand-held token)

3.   What you are (biometrics)

The FDIC took this step in recognition that single-threaded controls should be considered cybersecurity risk indicators, and more robust security measures reduce risk. The Account-Hijacking FDIC publication prompted the development of a number of alternatives for the second authentication factor. For example, security questions and device recognition technologies have all since been designed and implemented in an attempt to create defense-in-depth at the consumer level.[20] Since then, many companies have adopted two-factor authentication as the standard for authentication from external sites. Two-factor authentication is a stronger control than single-factor authentication.

However, although the second authentication factor strengthens the user authentication to the defense-in-depth layer protected by it, it does not provide additional controls for any of the subsequent infrastructure layers. Even if the Equifax website was protected by two-factor authentication, it was at the application layer, and the Apache Struts vulnerability allowed access to the operating system, so it would have allowed the same bypass.

Financial firms must assume successful attacks will occur at each layer, and engineer controls are designed to ensure that authentication cannot be achieved from one layer to the next by people or processes that are not explicitly and individually authorized to specific resources at both levels. This way, the weak link in the chain does not break security because the authorized access path and corresponding expected control points on either side of the break continuously uphold data flow.

The odds of a successful attack are therefore reduced to the probability of a successful attack at all layers. Mathematically, the probability of a successful attack in a pure defense-in-depth model, wherein any one weak link in the chain can compromise the whole, are calculated as in Figure 4-4. As any single vulnerability can expose the entire chain, the attack with the highest probability of success tends to dominate the result. That is, all insiders have authorized access to the network and anyone with authorized access to the network is in a position to launch an attack.

```
Probability ("P") of Attack Success =
P(Workstation) = 1 – as everyone has access to their own
workstation
* Max  {
          Max {
                    P(Network) = 1 IF internal network admin attacker
                    P(Network Vulnerability)
          }
          Max {
                    P(Operating System) = 1 – IF internal OS admin
attacker
                    P(OS Vulnerability) – IF internal attacker
                    P(Network) *  P(OS Vulnerability) – IF external
attackers
          }
          Max {
                    P(Application) = 1 – IF internal application support
attackers,
                    P(Application Vulnerability)
          }
          Max {
                    P(Database) = 1 – IF internal database admin
attacker
                    P(Database Vulnerability) – IF internal attacker
                    P(Network) * (Database Vulnerability) – IF external
attacker
          }
}
```

Figure 4-4. *Probability of successful attack: all layers network-accessible*

Note that Figure 4-4 does not take damage into consideration but simply acknowledges that a successful attack is possible. For example, in the absence of compensating controls that limit full network access to people who are authorized network administrators, anyone with a workstation on the network does not need to breach the network layer to attack an operating system directly. Figure 4-5 shows the probability calculation that instead supposes that strict interlayer tollgates are in place, whereby one would actually have to breach network security to attempt an operating system attack and would need to breach operating system security to launch an application attack, and so on. The concept of defense-in-depth intuitively calls to mind this supposition that such a conditional probability is appropriate, but given its porous layer assumptions, this type of odds calculation is rarely strictly applied.

```
Probability ("P") of Attack Success =
{
  P(Workstation) = 1
   *  MAX {
       P(Network) = 1 (if net admin)
       P(Network Vulnerability)
       }
   *  MAX {
       P(OS) = 1 (if OS admin)
       P(OS Vulnerability)
       }
    *  MAX {
       P(Application) = 1 (if App Supp)
       P(Application Vulnerability)
       }
   *  MAX {
       P(Database) = 1  (if DB admin)
       P(Database Vulnerability)
       }
}
```

Figure 4-5. *Probability of successful attack: layers accessible in order*

The Next Evolution

Figure 4-6 estimates some initial odds of successful attack, then fills in the math corresponding to the calculations in Figures 4-4 and 4-5. Note the exemplar probabilities were chosen as relative to each other, reflective of the financial industry. The brief rationale for each is that (1) network periphery typically gets the most attention (10 percent); (2) there are typically several versions of operating systems, and sometimes it is hard for admins to keep track of control parameters (50 percent); (3) applications change so much more than other environments that they are at much higher risk for zero day threats (75 percent); and (4) database management systems often have constraints that make integration with legacy systems difficult without some known security exposure (60 percent).

Attacker:	External	Internal	NW Admin	OS Admin	App Support	DB Admin	NW&OS
Probability of Attack Success Case (a):							
P(Workstation)	100%	100%	100%	100%	100%	100%	100%
Network	10%	10%	100%	10%	10%	10%	100%
Operating System	5%	50%	50%	100%	50%	50%	100%
Application	75%	75%	75%	75%	100%	75%	75%
Database	6%	60%	60%	60%	60%	100%	60%
OVERALL PROBABILITY FOR ROLE:	**75%**	**75%**	**100%**	**100%**	**100%**	**100%**	**100%**
Probability of Attack Success Case (b):							
P(Workstation)	100%	100%	100%	100%	100%	100%	100%
Network	10%	10%	100%	10%	10%	10%	100%
Operating System	**5%**	**5%**	50%	100%	**5%**	**5%**	100%
Application	**4%**	**4%**	**38%**	75%	100%	**4%**	75%
Database	**2%**	**2%**	**23%**	**45%**	60%	100%	**45%**
OVERALL PROBABILITY FOR ROLE:	**10%**	**10%**	100%	100%	100%	100%	100%

Figure 4-6. *Comparison of calculation results*

Note that the cell intersecting the *Internal User* row, *Probability of Attack Success Case (a)* column, shows the base case vulnerability probability in each layer, as that user may be expected to have direct network connection to all layers, but no privilege in any of them. This also assumes strict segregation of access for environments, wherein Operating System Administrators do not have access to database configurations or processes. However, because administrative roles are sometimes combined, the last column in Figure 4-6 demonstrates that probability of successful attack will increase when this occurs.

Bold numbers in Figure 4-6 for the Figure 4-4 calculations are the odds of successful attack that assumes that once on the internal network, attacks can bridge layers. Bold numbers in Figure 4-6 for the Figure 4-5 calculations (wherein layers have to be breached in sequence) highlight those that differ from the odds using the Figure 4-4 method. Although administrators would still have an advantage in producing successful attacks, the calculations show that the probability that they could do so on a given layer is drastically reduced. Moreover, the ability for an external attacker or an internal non-privileged user is dramatically reduced both overall and for individual layers.

Circle back to our observation that the set of situations in which there will be a cyber attack is the intersection of the set of systems in which there are vulnerabilities with a set of the situations in which an attacker chooses to exploit vulnerability. If the Apache Struts vulnerability was the exemplar Application vulnerability with the probability of 75 percent, then Figure 4-6 shows that, with layered controls, we can reduce the conditional probability at the left side of the equation so that it becomes a less attractive attack target because the odds of successful exploit are reduced.

$$P(cyberattack_s) = P(application\ vulnerability_s) *$$
$$P(exploit_s | application\ vulnerability_s)$$

$$= 0.75 * 0.10$$

$$= 0.075 = 7.5\%$$

Because of the weak-link-in-the-chain analogy, focus on authentication controls to protect defense layers has long been known to be inadequate to reduce the odds of successful cybersecurity attack. Preventive control is just one element of a successful cybersecurity program that requires a *closed-loop* system (as opposed to a linear one that is designed to simply thwart attacks). As illustrated in Figure 4-7, a closed loop system prompts continuous improvement of the defense strategy. In the early days of cybersecurity, this closed-loop flow was (and still may be) described as the Prevent, Detect, Recover, or "PDR," loop. The idea is to start with the best fortification possible to prevent intruders. But at the same time, fully understand that it may not be possible to protect against them, so prepare to detect their presence.

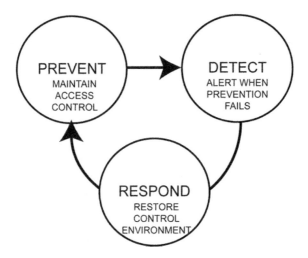

Figure 4-7. *PDR loop*

Also understand that if, despite the best prevention and detection efforts, an attack is successful, the firm will need to recover, so organizations should prepare in parallel for that situation as well. This approach was adopted from a more traditional *first responder* motto among police, fire, and emergency medical professionals who similarly follow a PDR loop. These groups also try to prevent harm, but where harm cannot be avoided, they strive be able to detect it and respond swiftly and effectively. The law enforcement community was actually the main driver behind the creation of computer forensic techniques that led to the development of the first cybersecurity control that has the ability to detect an attack in progress and respond by neutralizing the threat (Norton Antivirus).[21] Various versions of the PDR loop have been floating around the Information Security community for decades.[22] Today's PDR loops encompass automated monitoring at all defense-in-depth levels and combine both automated and human responses. Where detection and response are effective, the odds of a successful attack will be reduced, as even successful authentication by attackers can be terminated before they have enough time to achieve an attack goal.

To fully appreciate the sophistication of today's PDR loops, it is helpful to understand the influence of a variant of the closed-loop defense concept that comes from military history, which emphasizes not just the ability to detect lapses in existing controls but also to detect the potential impact of evolving external activities on a system of interest. That perspective has its origination in air force fighter plane strategy, which relies heavily on situational awareness in the context of enemy behavior. The loop has four stages: observe, orient, decide, act ("OODA"), in which security depends on the ability to assess the current environment in the context of the threat and the mission and to use that assessment to alter mission strategy in real time.[23] The PDR and OODA loops have heavily influenced systemic approaches to systems security engineering and are shown in Figure 4-8.

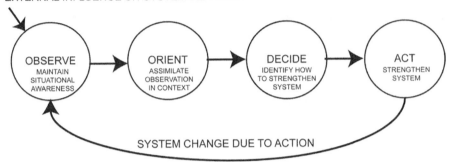

Figure 4-8. *OODA loop*

Shown in Figure 4-9 is the most recent addition to the closed-loop strategy for containing cybersecurity threats, which has in the past few years been codified by the US National Institute of Standards and Technology as a five-stage Cybersecurity Framework: Identify, Protect, Detect, Respond, and Recover. The framework includes emphasis on governance and culture as critical aids in organizing information, enabling risk management decisions, addressing threats, and improving defenses by learning from previous activities. The focus on closed-loops fosters recognition that the only way to maintain low odds of successful cybersecurity attack is for the system itself to evolve with each new threat and attack pattern.

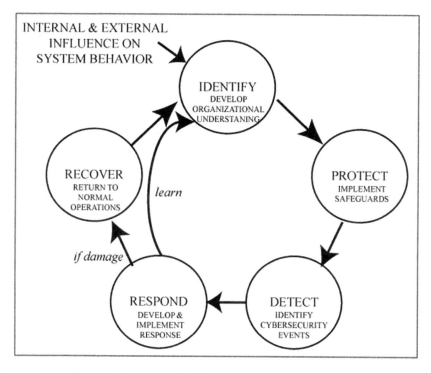

Figure 4-9. *NIST cybersecurity loop*

This approach to cybersecurity risk is consistent with the advice of Taleb in the book *Antifragile,* where he explained that, while it is not possible to measure the likelihood of an event that does not currently exist, it is nevertheless always possible to measure the capabilities of a given environment to respond to threats.[24] Where one environment can be shown to increase in strength in the face of adverse events, and another simply has the ability to be rebuilt, you can state with confidence that the former environment is less fragile than the latter one, should a cybersecurity event occur. This concept is explored more deeply later in this book.

97

Although it seems clear that such evolutionary approaches to cybersecurity control will reduce the odds of successful attack, the more holistic the control, the harder it is to put numbers on the odds. Again circling back to our observation that the set of situations in which there will be a cyberattack is the intersection of the set of systems in which there are vulnerabilities with a set of the situations in which an attacker chooses to exploit vulnerability, recall that the way to reduce the odds of cyberattack is to reduce the probability of vulnerability.

Although it is not possible to anticipate every software security bug or design flaw, it is possible to anticipate that every automated control will one day have one. The trick is to understand and drive down the left side of the equation, to customize it so that it becomes a less attractive attack target because the odds of successful exploit are reduced. The message of Figure 4-9 is that if failures in critical controls can be quickly detected, even if the vulnerability is exploited, a quick detection and response can make it less likely that the vulnerability will result in a successful cyberattack. For example, assume a large bank had configured the network periphery to detect when external IP address connected to the network periphery and to automate a query to all two-factor authentication systems to verify that the user at the address had authenticated using strong authentication. Suppose further that, in the event the automated query was unsuccessful in finding a match, the network connection would be automatically dropped and referred to a security operations team for investigation. This rapid response would have reduced the time an intruder spent on the network to seconds and would have drastically reduced the odds of successful achievement of attack objectives. The network vulnerability originally had a probability of 10 percent, and Figure 4-6 shows that even with layered controls, it remains at 10 percent. However, with detective controls, we can reduce the conditional probability at the left side of the equation to reflect the fact that the duration of the connection would further reduce the chance for attack, and it would not be an understatement to estimate that the probability of success would reduce to 0.1 percent for external attacks. The equation would change to this:

$$P(cyberattack_S) = P(networkvulnerability_S) *$$
$$P(exploit_S | networkvulnerability_S)$$

$$= 0.10 * 0.001$$

$$= 0.0001 = 0.01\%$$

To use this type of odds estimation, there are two critical factors for success in the endeavor that will require consensus and governance. One is technical, the other cultural. The technical hurdle is an agreed-upon method for estimating the probability that controls will be vulnerable. Judgment must be relative to the strength of controls within the target environment, and that is hard to estimate, so parameters must be developed to aid in the estimation. It is acceptable to differ across organizations as long as the estimation method is consistent when one probability is compared with another. The team developing the estimation protocol should focus on gathering enough parameters with which to evaluate controls that allow relative comparison and also use common sense.

Remember there is no industry consensus on absolute vulnerability measures. But there has, however, been a range of potential measurement techniques published that could fill its own book. Organizations can make use of industry standards where applicable, and follow best practices as they evolve. For example, organizations can follow CERT guidelines for evaluating the potential for software vulnerabilities.[25] For another example, authentication strength may be measured in factors, but the relative strength of factors changes over time as new tools and techniques develop for both control and exploit, so any estimation of probability of internal controls will need to be periodically revisited.

The second critical factor for success in odds estimation is cultural. It is very difficult for those who design and operate controls to participate in projects that make them redundant. Where a strong chain of two-factor authentication technologies protects the network perimeter, it may seem like a waste of time to be searching databases for evidence to the contrary. To really reduce the odds of cyber attack using detective measures, control engineers and operators must willingly suspend their beliefs that the existing controls actually work. They must also be comfortable enough in the control design that automated termination of processes that appear to bypass them is not only justified, but plain common sense.

Although there may be no single best approach for measuring the odds of a breach, or even being attacked, there are probability-based methods that can enhance situational awareness. Adoption of somewhat incomplete models, and acceptance of uncertainty, can still provide general benefits as even imperfect estimates may provide valuable indicators. Increased availability of event data, improved analytical techniques, and overall improvements of incident transparency may begin moving the industry away from the age of plausible deniability. More and more observers of cyber breaches adopt views similar to that of the Pennsylvania Attorney General, who said of the Equifax case: "Unfortunately, our corporate culture has swung so far in the direction of valuing profits above people that Equifax's behavior, while appalling, is not surprising."[26]

Moving Ahead

The first four chapters have examined considerations related to noticing, measuring, and estimating cybersecurity risk dimensions in financial institutions. The focus shifts in upcoming chapters toward opportunities, and challenges, in acting about risk observations. The next chapter explores potential response actions, to begin to explore what management can and should do in response to recognized risks.

Notes

1. Securosis Blog 2009. http://securosis.com/ blog/an-open-letter-to-robert-carr-ceo-of-heartland-payment-systems, 8/12/2009.

2. Bernstein, Peter, *Against the Gods, The Remarkable Story of Risk* (Hoboken, NJ: John Wiley and Sons, 1996), p. 334.

3. FICO stands for Fair Isaac Corporation, the FIC score is that corporation's flagship product, www.fico.com.

4. FDIC's Credit Card Activities Manual, Chapter 8: Scoring and Modeling, https://www.fdic.gov/ regulations/examinations/credit_card/

5. Ibid.

6. Computer System Security and Privacy Advisory Board (CSSPAB) Meeting and Workshop on Approaches to Measuring Security, June 13, 2000. See author contribution: Information Security Metrics, An Audit-based Approach at: http:// bayuk.com/publications/BayukNIST.pdf

7. https://www.fsisac.com/article/fs-isac-announces-formation-financial-systemic-analysis-resilience-center-fsarc

8. Open Security Foundation, DataLossDB, http://
    www.datalossdb.org/ DataLossDB was founded in
    2005 and distributed available cybersecurity data
    loss incident data from August 2008 until mid-2015,
    providing unbiased, high quality data regarding
    data loss events. In 2015, the effort was taken private
    by its founders and data subsequent to 2015 may
    be purchased from VulnDB at https://vulndb.
    cyberriskanalytics.com.

9. Verizon Enterprise. (2017). "2017 Data Breach
    Investigations Report, 10th Edition."

10. Ibid, Appendix D.

11. Krebs, B., "WannaCry Ransomware," in *Krebs on
    Security*, https://krebsonsecurity.com/tag/
    wanna-cry-ransomware/, May 13, 2017.

12. Rittel, H.W.J. and Webber, M.M., Dilemmas in a
    general theory of planning. *Policy Sciences*, 1973.
    4(2): pp. 155-169.

13. Geer, D. "Re: discussion topic for Mini-Metricon 5.5
    Metricon Program Committee Communication,"
    11/1/2010.

14. Verizon Enterprise. (2017). "2017 Data Breach
    Investigations Report, 10th Edition."

15. Bryan-Low, C. (2005). Identity Thieves Organize.
    Wall Street Journal.

16. BITS (2011). Malware Risks and Mitigation. www.
    bitsinfo.org, The Financial Services Roundtable.

17. Krebs, B. (2017). "Ayuda! (Help!) Equifax Has My Data!" *Krebs on Security*.

18. Matthew Goldstein et.al. (2014). Neglected Server Provided Entry for JPMorgan Hackers. *New York Times*. https://dealbook.nytimes.com/2014/12/22/entry-point-of-jpmorgan-data-breach-is-identified/

19. Bayuk, Jennifer L. *Stepping Through the InfoSec Program*, (Schaumberg, IL: ISACA, 2007), p. 24.

20. FDIC (December 14, 2004). Putting an End to Account-Hijacking Identity Theft, Federal Deposit Insurance Corporation Division of Supervision and Consumer Protection Technology Supervision Branch.

21. Schmidt, Howard. . *Patrolling Cyberspace*, (Blue Bell, PA: Larstan Publishing, 2006).

22. Bayuk, Jennifer L.. *Enterprise Security for the Executive: Setting the Tone at the Top,* (Westport, CT: Praeger, 2010) chapter 3: Triad and True.

23. Boyd, J., *A discourse on winning and losing, in Briefing slides*. 1987, Air University Library Document No. M-U 43947: Maxwell Air Force Base, AL. Note: this is the seminal presentation that is frequently used to introduce the concept an Observe-Orient-Device-Act (OODA) Loop.

24. Taleb, Nassim Nicholas , *Antifragile: Things That Gain From Disorder*, (New York: Random House, 2012).

25. https://www.cert.org/cybersecurity-
     engineering/

26. Shapiro, Josh, "Viewpoints," *The Philadelphia
     Enquirer*, September 28. 2017: http://www.philly.
     com/philly/opinion/commentary/equifax-data-
     breach-cyber-security-josh-shapiro-20170926.
     html

CHAPTER 5

What Can We Do?

The previous chapters have served as evidence that cybersecurity risk to financial institutions is largely, perhaps almost entirely, viewed as a potential *negative* impact the event may have. Although standards vary slightly on the definition, it is generally acknowledged the outcome of any risk event can be considered positive or negative, depending on the viewer's perspective. In a gamble between two players, both may consider the bet an opportunity, but once the outcome is known, the loser becomes keenly aware they have taken a risk.

Delivering services over the internet provides substantial business opportunity but is, of course, *inherently* risky. Inherent, as a modifier for risk, refers to the probability of a risk event in the absence of steps taken to treat the observed risk. To understand how true this is, simply spin up a single virtual machine from a cloud service provider, do not configure any firewalls or automated security patches, and watch the security logs. Almost instantly, previously unknown adversaries will target the machines. That is, any internet-connected device that is not actively protected can be assumed compromised. This inherent risk is managed by "treating" it. Risk treatment is a generic term that covers identifying, selecting, and executing options for reducing risk. An example of risk treatment in cybersecurity is a password, although this treatment does not eliminate the risk. Adding a password reduces inherent risk but leaves behind significant *residual* risk due to the ease internet predators can eavesdrop on network traffic and/or exploit other vulnerabilities that expose password strings in

P. Rohmeyer and J. L. Bayuk, *Financial Cybersecurity Risk Management*,
https://doi.org/10.1007/978-1-4842-4194-3_5

human-readable format. Inadequate controls may allow residual risk to be higher than levels deemed acceptable by the enterprise. To significantly reduce risk associated with dependency on the internet for operations to an acceptable residual level for financial services applications begins with answering a fundamental question: What can we do? Simply, we need to take action to design and implement risk treatments against recognized and suspected cybersecurity and technology risks.

Risk Treatment Across the Organization

Risk treatment represents the conversion of risk analysis results into action. Assuming the potential impacts, costs, and probabilities have been determined as discussed in previous chapters, decision makers ideally have accumulated the information needed to generate and evaluate alternative risk management decisions. Risk treatment approaches are commonly categorized along the following options:

- Avoidance
- Reduction
- Transference
- Acceptance

Avoidance

It's often possible to simply *avoid* situations that carry risk. An example is migration to hosted software under cloud or Software as a Service (SaaS) models, rather than trying to remediate outdated systems. It should be expected any cloud solution will have its own inherent risks and technical vulnerabilities; however, it is reasonable to assume a cloud service provider is cognizant that cybersecurity is a sign of product quality and is therefore willing to commit to a high level of cybersecurity control. As a result, the risk of the hosted alternative may be expected to be lower than struggling with legacy architecture. Service providers also are expected to commit to independent control reviews and to maintain system security to counter new risks over time. Architecture design and continuous development should ideally be approached with an eye toward avoiding reducing the potential for vulnerabilities by continuously migrating away from components flagged as risk concerns during risk assessment activities. Maintenance, of course, represents an ongoing concern in all systems, and the use of SaaS solutions essentially transfers most of the maintenance obligation to the service provider. Now, assuring the provider is actually performing required maintenance becomes another obligation, but it appears there is industry consensus that the trade-off of software maintenance for vendor oversight is often favorable from operational and economic perspectives. Note that maintenance is a technology control in itself with positive benefits for security, like patching, and the maintenance controls meant to reduce the highest probability risks can be prioritized for monitoring activity. Another example of avoiding risk is to avoid known threats to specific technologies. Avoidance may be possible in some circumstances by removing vulnerable architectural pathways that have a higher probability of exploit by an attacker (i.e. reduce attack surface). Thereby, avoidance may provide a reduction in overall risk exposure.

Reduction

Steps can be taken to reduce vulnerabilities, the likelihood of events, and/or the eventual consequences should a risk event occur.

Mitigation is a term sometimes used by the industry as essentially synonymous with reduction, but it generally reflects that the enterprise is taking specific action to reduce risk to allow them to proceed with a desired architecture design rather than changing architectural fundamentals to avoid risk. Mitigation can include tactics to reduce all dependency on vulnerable system elements. For example, we can mitigate software by patching to reduce total vulnerabilities, or we can mirror data storage devices to lessen the consequences (damage) should a risk event occur.

If, despite the implementation of generally accepted or regulatory required controls, residual risk still appears too high, a financial institution will face discrete, unique decisions on how to bring risk to an acceptable residual level. To some cybersecurity professionals, it may seem like the answers are a straightforward step-by-step process:

1. Describe the desired control improvement.

2. Write a request for information (RFI) for the solution, and send it to cybersecurity vendors and consultants.

3. Choose the best of the RFI responses.

4. Write a request for proposal (RFP) and send to a short list of vendors and consultants that have the best RFI responses.

5. Select the best solution from the RFP responses.

6. Implement, deploy, and operate the new solution.

This approach has had such widespread adoption in the industry that some cybersecurity departments rarely, if ever, actually collaborate on basics such as hardening operating systems configurations or developing patching strategies with their engineering counterparts. Rather, they simply have the system and network administrators install successive cybersecurity products and view the firm's infrastructure from the perspective of the security control consoles. In fact, in some financial institutions, the cybersecurity department's entire mission is relegated to the selection and deployment of cybersecurity products.

This may explain why so many financial institutions have installed layer upon layer of cybersecurity technologies across their operating environments. Examples include various types of firewalls, operating system hardening tools, single sign-on and multifactor authentication systems, entitlement servers, anti-virus, anti-phishing, anti-malware, proxy servers, black lists, white lists, network encryption, disk encryption, key management servers, virtual private networks, intrusion detection, intrusion prevention, content filters, wireless scanners, web application firewalls, source code scanners, vulnerability scanners. These and more cybersecurity technologies may be used in a single environment.

Cybersecurity products are designed to limit the attack surface of inherently vulnerable technologies in order to reduce the risk of operating the technology to provide financial services. In other words, they provide general mitigation benefits that can be applied to multiple system contexts. The rush to remediate newly discovered risks, and perhaps a lack of technical understanding of the nature of specific vulnerabilities, has created an environment wherein best practices dictate that even the smallest financial institutions should expect to find themselves owning extremely complex and interconnected layers of security architecture.

The result is what seems to be a never-ending cycle of spending evaluations. Moreover, acquisition of cyber tools is of course limited by budget constraints. Ironically, sometimes existing system configuration is a cheaper and more effective solution than purchasing a tool specifically to mitigate one type of attack; cybersecurity professionals refer to the latter approach as "bolt-on". Bolt-on approaches also inevitably raise operational support concerns, as the adoption of any new technology should be expected to result in the creation of new technical administration tasks, as well as produce additional knowledge requirements for support personnel. That means actual cost increases are always higher than the "ticket price" for the technology purchase, a factor often illustrated by total cost of ownership models. As most experienced technical operations managers recognize, the "soft" support costs for any new technology can be substantial and are often overlooked during acquisition.

Mitigation often takes the form of specialized controls architectures that represent new, non-functional system requirements for continued operation. Bolt-on controls reflect emerging operational realities that are often viewed as additions to systems architecture with the hope of providing extensible benefits.

Ideally, the controls architecture should be informed by risk analysis to carefully consider the need for changes in system design to minimize the attack surface. Where the use of new tools appear to be indicated, such analysis should also consider the tradeoff between changes in system architecture and deployment of security-specific technologies that fortify the system of interest against a small set of observed risks. In this approach, organizations tend to try to identify how previously installed technologies of all types may be reconfigured to provide risk reduction benefits to newly observed risks, thereby allowing the enterprise to avoid some new technology purchases.

As described previously in Chapter 4, one of the most critical cybersecurity controls is situational awareness. Even the best preventive technical controls may have hidden software vulnerabilities, and a determined adversary with insider knowledge may bypass even the most rigorous multi-factor authentication; therefore, the ability to detect attacks is a vital requirement to drive down risk. Anti-virus and intrusion detection tools are designed to detect known attack patterns and should be deployed precisely for that reason. They are also good starting points for training cybersecurity response teams on operational procedures. However, as sophisticated adversaries produce ever more insidious attacks, it is fast becoming financial industry standard to collect as much baseline data on user behavior as possible, with an eye toward leveraging "big data" analysis tools to identify abnormal behavior. Alerts generated from behavior that deviates from baseline may indicate there is an intruder in your midst. Intentional deviations from authorized behavior may be simulated to ensure these tools trigger properly, as part of "threat hunting" exercises.

Note there is no risk of violating privacy in this kind of user monitoring. The only users on a system at this level are individuals who are providing technology services to the firm doing the monitoring. Considerations such as these drive financial institutions to consider establish alerting capabilities on network traffic anomalies, file transfer anomalies, login pattern fail anomalies, and all sorts of behavior that may not qualify as an unauthorized event if performed by an authorized user but could be evidence of an intrusion. All such alerts can be effective indicators that potentially malicious behavior is occurring within a financial institution's technology environment. Alerts as well as employee or customer reports of incidents are key triggers that enable closed-loop cybersecurity operations methodologies to maximize value from the response capability. Even if an anomaly alert is a false alarm, it helps the cybersecurity response team better understand authorized activities, and so they become better able to differentiate false alarms from actual unauthorized event activities going forward.

The available array of cybersecurity technologies that purport to offer risk reduction is vast, complex, and ever-changing. The eager marketing and sales functions of the sizable cybersecurity vendor space adds to the excitement with a continuous stream of new capabilities. Enterprises spend considerable resources on scanning the environment for new cyber tools that may provide benefits to known and future risks. The evaluation process and related spending decisions have become continuous activities within the cybersecurity governance function.

Transfer

Where risk cannot readily be reduced, one non-technical alternative is to lessen risk by shifting risk ownership to another party via a process of risk transfer. Risk transfer strategy is commonly executed via contracts such as service level agreements with technology service providers, rapid technical escalation of suspected technology risk events, as well as cyber insurance.

The use of cyber insurance continues to become more common; however, the industry is still somewhat immature compared to other forms of insurance. There is real concern among potential cyber insurance customers that risk profiles upon which cyber insurance is based are not well-understood.[1] This may be because many insurance carriers are relatively new to the business of cybersecurity insurance, and their products are constantly evolving. There is also uncertainty on effective methods for pricing cyber policies. A study by the RAND Institute explored various approaches to policy pricing.[2] The RAND study observed a core challenge of a fundamental lack of publicly available data, inhibiting statistical analysis of the type historically completed in pricing other types of insurance. No surprise, the study found wide variability in degree of sophistication of techniques used for pricing, and other operational challenges such as assessing risk in third-party relationships.

Despite the apparent growing pains, some standard categories of cybersecurity insurance coverage have emerged. Policies are typically capped at a maximum monetary amount, but this amount may be just what is necessary to lower the risk of monetary loss to an acceptable residual level. Below are some currently available cybersecurity coverage options. Financial institutions considering insurance as an option should note that cyber insurance companies typically require some proof of adequate controls, such as independent control assessments, prior to issuing such policies.

- *Crisis Management:* Covers the cost of managing public relations and/or legal communication in case of a data breach. This may include call centers for potential victims to be included in crisis management coverage.

- *Data Loss and Restoration:* Covers the cost of restoring lost data. In some cases, coverage is also provided for the cost of diagnosing and repairing the cause of the loss of data. It is limited in terms of the cause of data loss and might have high retention fees.

- *Extortion:* Covers the cost of ransom in cases where hackers demand money for not disclosing the data publicly and/or not destroying data.

- *Forensic Investigation:* Covers the cost of determining the cause of loss of data.

- *Malicious Code:* Covers liability in cases where an institution has inadvertently allowed malicious software within its systems to escape and cause damage to the systems of others.

- *Privacy Liability Coverage:* Covers client losses due to loss of client identification information in cases of data breach. This may include notification costs for all parties (even if they are not clients) whose data may have been compromised in the data breach. It may also include credit monitoring for impacted individuals or businesses.

- *Systems Interruption:* Covers business lost due to an interruption in systems operation and/or expenses incurred due to the loss of systems.

- *Theft and Fraud:* Covers expenses related to the theft of data or funds.

Risk transfer can be accomplished through multiple means, as risk observed within a single system can be transferred to multiple parties. A combined approach may be useful in overcoming some of the current shortcomings in pricing and risk assessment models used by the insurers. The use of cyber insurance "towers" can be instrumental in this regard, by carefully buying a variety of coverage types that broadens the effective scope of coverage while spreading the risk across multiple carriers.[3] The combination of well-written service level agreements and the purchase of multiple cyber insurance policies could be effective in providing substantial risk transfer benefits.

Acceptance

A frequently chosen option is to simply *accept* risk. Execution of risk treatment strategies can rarely (if ever) entirely eliminate risk, and so decision makers need to recognize they will always operate in an environment with some level of accepted cybersecurity risk.

Organizations may identify circumstances, however, where they decide to not treat specific instances of risk. In some financial institutions, it is possible that managers at various levels in the organizational hierarchy to have flexibility to accept risk within their own domain of technology responsibility. Executives who allow this type of decentralized risk decision making should understand the more interconnected and interdependent financial services become, the more likely it is a risk acceptance decision by one part of the business may create risk for other connected parties. Risk acceptance by one party in an interconnected value chain may create the potential for cascading risk, where a negative event in the early stages of a process result in numerous "downstream" manifestations of the risk event. A simple example is if one organization allows uncontrolled network access to third parties, a cyber attack launched through the third-party could result in negative consequences on all connected enterprises.

Another complexity is the potential accumulation of risk, where individual risk acceptance decisions combine to form a greater, but perhaps not immediately visible, risk. For example, assume there is an organization where the administrators of systems architecture decide to reduce spending on vulnerability management (e.g., patch less frequently), thereby accepting a higher level of risk. Let's also assume elsewhere in the same organization there is an independent decision to reduce cyber spending by reducing the reliance on third-party security testing (e.g., test less frequently). The individual decisions represent clear acceptance of increased risk; however, the combination of the two risks should create a higher level of concern, as the individual acceptance decisions would result in the simultaneous weakening of preventive (patching) and detective (technical testing) aspects, and as a result this would create a more substantial, comprehensive concern.

As a result, it is rapidly becoming best practice that, even in situations where risk acceptance is distributed, individual risk acceptance decisions are centrally reported and independently reviewed by a risk management function. Acceptance should be even more closely monitored where compelling business opportunities or customer demands necessitate acceptance of otherwise intolerable cybersecurity risk.

Risk Treatment Across the Enterprise Architecture

The execution of risk treatment strategies can be analyzed by considering treatments as they impact specific aspects of enterprise architecture. Gartner Group described the concept of Enterprise Architecture as "a discipline for proactively and holistically leading enterprise responses to disruptive forces by identifying and analyzing the execution of change toward desired business vision and outcomes."[4] Various models of enterprise architecture emphasize major organizational domains of people, processes, and technologies.[5] The enterprise context is explored in further detail later in this book.

Treatment strategies can be executed by developing implementation plans across the enterprise architecture. Table 5-1 is matrix that illustrates sample tactics that correspond treatment strategies with major architectural domains.

Table 5-1. *Treatment Approaches Across the Enterprise*

	Risk Treatments for Insider Threat		
	People	*Processes*	*Technologies*
Avoid	Automate decisions made by people to ensure there is no subjectively in the result.	Require human supervisor to approve high risk transactions.	Do not allow high risk transactions from mobile devices.
Reduce	Increase monitoring of the use of privileged user accounts.	Design business flows to minimize data transfer and encrypt where possible.	Restrict the provisioning of privileged credentials.
Transfer	Use third-party consulting or temp service to replace employees and require them by contract to pay for consequences of their employee misbehavior.	Write contracts that require counterparties to accept risk of monetary loss due to business process failure.	Purchase cyber insurance for highly vulnerable technical architectures.

After completing an analysis similar to Table 5-1 (and ensuring all potential options are regulatory compliant), treatment approaches can be aligned with specific enterprise domains to move the organization closer to execution. For example, people and process objectives, such as improving the prioritization of monitoring privileged user accounts, will provide concrete requirements for specific technology control designs such as the integration of enhanced monitoring and alerting capabilities. The ability to drill down (e.g., "avoidance" posture is broken into People, Process, and Technology tactics) and then back up as needed informs decision making by demonstrating the alignment of individual controls decisions with a particular risk treatment posture.

A customized version of Table 5-1 can be useful to identify potential gaps in treatment strategies and can therefore identify opportunities to strengthen risk treatment. For example, there is common recognition that risk, and ultimate accountability, cannot be outsourced. The result is a pressing need for effective third-party monitoring and oversight of outsourced systems and processes. However, some third-party risk can potentially be transferred via the use of well-designed service level agreements that include monetary penalties for risk events or perhaps establish contractual requirements for vendor cybersecurity architecture and practices. Similarly, cyber insurance coverage can be extended to include coverage for events caused by third-party action or inaction. As a result, the broad treatment strategy for treating third-party risk could be crafted to include elements of continuous oversight, service level requirements, and cyber insurance. Similarly, prioritization of the "people" domain may be appropriate where perhaps advanced persistent threat (APT) risks are viewed as "high" within the risk assessment, and so multiple treatments can be designed to execute avoidance, reduction, and transfer strategies, thereby providing comprehensive and redundant controls.

Yet another potential benefit of conducting a treatment analysis using a structure such as Table 5-1 is it can provide an at-a-glance view of the relative strengths of redundant treatment options. For example, in the analysis of social media risks, there may be an indication to prioritize treatments related to phishing risks. This includes the deployment of technology treatments such as e-mail filtering and the disabling/ stripping of http links within messages but also people treatments such as investment in user awareness training. Process changes could be made as well, such as automating workflows within applications rather than continuing reliance on e-mail exchange. The inherent strengths and weaknesses of the respective approaches become clear in a breakdown such as that of Table 5-1. Awareness training essentially represents asking, pleading, or begging users to determine indicators of "suspicious" links, then remaining vigilant as to not click on anything deemed "suspicious." Technology-based treatments like restricting browser activity to sandbox virtual machines that have no access to the internal network, in contrast, are inherently stronger controls as they function scientifically rather than attempting to overcome shortcomings in human cognition and attention spans. As a result, analysis such as that in Table 5-1 can be useful in helping the enterprise to identify opportunities for architectural improvement by, perhaps, shifting funding away from awareness training toward anti-phishing technologies over time. Despite hefty investment in awareness training, the delivery of malicious code via phishing remains frequent and we can expect adversaries will continue to employ such methods. A shift in prioritization of technology-based treatments for phishing threats seems to be in order. More generally, we can use analyses such as Table 5-1 to identify relative weaknesses in treatments and illustrate potential alternatives across all architectural domains.

Executing on Risk Treatment Decisions

The earlier discussion is mostly hypothetical as it explains potential courses of action with respect to planning cybersecurity risk treatment strategies across the enterprise. As explained earlier, formulation of treatment alternatives can be informed by the risk assessment. Many risk assessment approaches, in fact, end with recommendations phrased as identification of treatments, followed by calculation of post-treatment residual risk. Like all risk management strategies, though, such recommendations are of little value without accompanying analysis that lead to the choices from identified alternatives that includes effective implementation execution. Execution can sometimes be restricted or delayed by factors such as the availability of human resources or funding. However, the move to action sometimes comes down to attaining an appropriate level of organizational motivation. A number of common motivators are seen throughout the financial services industry, including the following:

- *Legal and regulatory requirements:* Most enterprises have developed enterprise-wide capabilities for rapid reaction to new legal and regulatory requirements. This includes various oversight, audit, and committee functions that create an organizational funnel to capture regulatory advances and move them swiftly into the view of leadership.

- *Regulatory direction:* Organizations may be motivated to execute treatment strategies when regulators provide "early warning" of the upcoming emergence of new regulations or new interpretations of old regulations. Items marked as "comments" in one exam should be reclassified as "findings" in the subsequent cycle if not corrected, providing the opportunity for action before negative reports are presented.

- *Fear of financial loss:* The potential of financial damage can often move management into action with particular vigor thanks to the threat of real money losses.

- *Fear of reputational damage:* Marketplace reactions to the news of breaches have in some cases been substantial, and management arguably could be motivated to avoid such outcomes.

- *Board or Audit Committee mandate:* A combination of factors may drive Board and Audit Committee members to enact mandates that can have a motivating effect on project execution.

It is important to note, however, that despite the existence of functional compliance regimes and internal governance, motivation does not always effectively continue to the execution level. An example is despite the existence of data breach notification laws in most US states for many years, and the incorporation of said laws within enterprise policies and procedures, the execution of breach notification is triggered only by the willingness of technical staff to declare a suspicious event a "breach." A systems administrator, for instance, may make a personal decision to not report an obvious breach because they fear direct, personal consequences, regardless of the fact they would place the organization into non-compliance. The criteria to declare certain observations to be breach events are under consideration in the context of European Union Global Data Protection Regulation (GDPR) requirements for timely breach reporting to authorities. Both the US and EU breach reporting regulations hinge on the willful compliance of technical staff and may therefore not move enterprises into actual compliance. In other words, treatments based on an assumption of employee cooperation may be *practically ineffective* even though *compliance* can be documented. Regulators seek widespread adoption of best practices to provide broad risk treatment in theory, but only the enterprise can execute on treatment strategies to drive positive outcomes.

Validating Effectiveness in Execution

This chapter has provided a comprehensive overview of the types of treatment strategies one can implement to reduce cybersecurity risk. Organizations need to decide how to measure control effectiveness as they embark on execution of risk treatment strategies. The only way to do that is to envision a state where risk reduction is achieved and measure attributes of that state. Only this type of measure can validate that a control actually works.

Once the future state is in place, it is also important to know whether the controls were actually implemented as planned, or if validation metrics reflect risk reduction for some other reason. It is also important to devise measures that verify controls are implemented as designed. These are verification metrics. Always remember that control measures and metrics are not the same as risk reduction or risk metrics. Control metrics measure cybersecurity capability, not risk. Validation metrics may reveal heightened risk even though verification metrics show all controls are fully operating as designed. Risk analysis should be an ongoing process that considers changes in both the internal and external environment.[6]

There is a common cliché that cyber risk treatment is largely about the need to simply not be "the slowest antelope in the herd," and so there is no need to spend to be best in class, or the fastest antelope. The type of animal may change occasionally depending on who tells the story; however, the declaration remains that as long as you are better prepared than the least prepared in your group you probably will not be the victim.

The continuous emergence of threats of increasing sophistication should serve to relegate this line of thinking to the archives. A variety of characteristics present organizations as attractive targets to the persistent adversary who takes intelligent and thoughtful steps to penetrate a target organization. Attackers today commonly appear to act without regard to how their target compares to the herd. Speedy and mediocre antelopes, as well as the slowest, are therefore all potential prey (Figure 5-1).

Figure 5-1. *The fastest antelope*

The antelope metaphor also illustrates limitations in the use of transfer as a cybersecurity risk treatment option because if the risk event is catastrophic, the existence of insurance, service level agreements, and vendor oversight reports will be of little value.

In other words, if the enterprise is irreparably harmed, the hope of a future insurance payout to breach response costs will provide little solace. Furthermore, a dangerous possibility to consider is overreliance on risk transfer via cyber insurance could potentially result in enterprises accepting higher levels of risk, as they believe they are "covered" by insurance. Enterprises, as well as auditors and regulators, need to realize it is certainly much easier to buy cyber insurance than it is to design and implement effective controls architectures. Shifting funds to increase cyber insurance coverage to generate better risk metrics could lead organizations to ignore the real-world impact of significant breaches. Residual risk calculations may therefore be more realistic if they are calculated before and after application of insurance and transfer benefits. It's safe to assume the antelope would be more interested in knowing its pre-insurance residual risk before embarking on its next journey and would probably not be terribly interested in the post-incident payout levels.

Moving Ahead

Earlier chapters illustrated risk characteristics in the context faced by most financial institutions and techniques to observe and measure important risk aspects. This chapter introduced the concept of risk treatment, reflecting potential management action resulting from improved understanding of risks faced by the institution. The result of successive risk treatment decisions is an increasingly complex controls architecture that presents substantial operational challenges. The next chapter considers the challenges associated with trying to manage the enterprise cybersecurity controls environment in an environment of continuously shifting risk dimensions.

Notes

1. "Why 27% of U.S. Firms Have No Plans to Buy Cyber Insurance." *Insurance Journal*, May 31, 2017, retrieved December 2017 from: *https://www.insurancejournal.com/news/national/2017/05/31/452647.htm*.

2. Romano Sky, Ablon, Kuehn, Jones *Content Analysis of Cyber Insurance Policies: How do Carriers Price Cyber Risk?* (Santa Monica, CA: RAND Corporation, 2017). https://www.rand.org/content/dam/rand/pubs/working_papers/WR1200/WR1208/RAND_WR1208.pdf

3. Ayers, E. (2015) Higher and higher: Cyber insurance towers take careful construction. *Advisen.* https://www.advisenltd.com/2015/09/24/higher-and-higher-cyber-insurance-towers-take-careful-construction/

4. Gartner Group (2018) Enterprise Architecture Definition, retrieved from https://www.gartner.com/it-glossary/enterprise-architecture-ea

5. Institute of Industrial and Systems Engineers (IISE) (2018). People, Process, Technology – The Three Elements For A Successful Organizational Transformation. Retrieved from http://www.iise.org/Details.aspx?id=24456

6. Bayuk, J.L., (2013) Security as a theoretical attribute construct, *Computers & Security* https://doi.org/10.1016/j.cose.2013.03.006

CHAPTER 6

How Do I Manage This?

Cybersecurity risk is ubiquitous and so there is a need to manage it as such, at the enterprise level. Management strategy begins with an understanding of business fundamentals: mission, vision, and core values. These fundamentals are not simply part of management strategy; they comprise the success criteria to which strategy itself is compared. Management strategy lays out detailed business objectives that correspond to goals, and develops plans for how they will be achieved. As an organization makes business plans, risk is a key consideration in evaluating and selecting from alternative management strategies. Decision makers need to recognize the technology associated with any business strategy may be exposed to cyberattack. Cybersecurity risk management at the level of the enterprise therefore begins with understanding and communicating how technology supports strategy. The structure and function of the *enterprise governance function* provide the key linkage to enable organizations to execute strategy; effective governance guides the movement of the organization toward strategic goals.

© Paul Rohmeyer, Jennifer L. Bayuk 2019
P. Rohmeyer and J. L. Bayuk, *Financial Cybersecurity Risk Management*,
https://doi.org/10.1007/978-1-4842-4194-3_6

Governance Operating Model

Strategic plans include allocation of activities to individuals in the form of roles and responsibilities and associated governance structures. It is important to recognize that it makes sense to use these enterprise management tools to directly manage the cybersecurity program, which is intended to model and support the execution of cyber strategy. However, consideration of cybersecurity from a strategic perspective is relatively new thinking. It is all too common to instead delegate the function to a group off to the side, whose role is to identify and fix security issues. These disconnected units tend to create piecemeal solutions without the full support of the management team whose buy-in is ultimately necessary for integration of cybersecurity risk management with enterprise risk management (ERM). A more integrated approach presents obvious efficiencies.

Governance is a general term that refers to both the process and outcome of good management—as Drucker and Deming pupils would say, "management by observation and control"[1] or "plan-do-study-act."[2] In financial services organizations, however, it may sometimes seem as though governance functions separately from management. This could be due to the array of requirements from different regulatory agencies and internal control divisions that make it very difficult for leadership to maintain situational awareness. "Governance" is also often the label given to a group that is charged with making sure that no requirements are missed. As cybersecurity is one of, if not the most, highly regulated part of technology, it is not unusual to devote special governance forums to it, as well as to have executives charged with policy and programs that run independently of the rest of the firm's risk management functions. Acknowledging it is not the forte of most cybersecurity professionals to run businesses; it is probably not appropriate to delegate business risk evaluation to cybersecurity experts. However, it is also not productive to allow cybersecurity risk management efforts exclusive of consideration of non-technical aspects of operational risk.

Ideally, governance in cybersecurity should be to business leadership as umpires are to coaches. Leaders and coaches agree to the rules, or at least on the sources of rules to which they are subject. These sources will be both regulatory and business-driven, both within and outside of leadership's control. Where cybersecurity risk is considered alongside business risk, there will be governance umpires who observe and report on cybersecurity policy and regulatory violations. Although the existence of good umpires may not necessarily produce good outcomes, a lack of umpires in cybersecurity, as in sports, is clearly a recipe for chaos. In the case of financial technology, rival team activities and scores are rarely visible, so governance umpires may seem more like Olympic judges in areas like skiing, where it is important not only to cross the line but to follow a well-defined path and avoid hitting obstacles along the way. In this role, as in Olympic sports, judges are sometimes mistrusted, bias may be suspected, replays may be required, and panels may be convened to adjudicate disputes. Similar scrutiny in matters of cyber governance could strengthen the cybersecurity program and ensure it has appropriate business focus.

It may appear to outside observers that financial regulatory examiners are the ultimate industry umpires. But in truth, the regulators do not have the capacity to make observations in all situations where they may be rules violations, so they rely on the institution's governance teams to establish monitoring and present metrics that demonstrate that regulations are followed. Internal and external auditors serve to provide assurance that governance processes are comprehensive enough to maintain regulatory compliance. As a result, when regulators identify a gap in compliance, it is reasonable to assume the observed gap is highly visible within the institution as well.

Governance teams may be expected to both publish all relevant rules and to keep statistics on every player. This is where the sports analogy begins to fall apart. Unlike sports, a financial services governance team typically cannot disqualify a player for not following the rules.

Only the leadership team can do that. Organizational leaders are the *actual* governors. Furthermore, leadership may be greatly influenced by enterprise customers, as leadership sets strategy and executes ostensibly in a way to satisfy the customer as part of their mission to drive enterprise value. Moreover they can set their own governance rules via published strategies for meeting business objectives. These factors create cybersecurity challenges in addition to those set by regulators, and the governance group has to ensure that roles and responsibilities ensure accountability for complying with them all.

Figure 6-1 illustrates a governance-operating model that is compliant with OCC standards for risk governance frameworks in large financial institutions. Smaller institutions are also expected to use OCC standards as guidelines when they create their own programs. The governance-operating model includes three layers of organizational structure: board of directors (BoD), governance committees, and executives. The BoD sets direction on strategy and provides guidance. Management creates governance committees to oversee day-to-day operations. The charters of these committees include organizational participants and are collectively intended to establish oversight of all roles and responsibilities related to fiduciary and social responsibility for the financial institution. In any such governance structure, risk management merits specific executive leadership. As the OCC put it: Guidelines set forth the roles and responsibilities for front line units, independent risk management, and internal audit. These units are fundamental to the design and implementation of the Framework. They are often referred to as the 'three lines of defense' and, together, should establish an appropriate system to control risk taking. These units should keep the board of directors informed of the covered bank's risk profile and risk management practices to allow the board of directors to provide credible challenges to management's recommendations and decisions.[3]

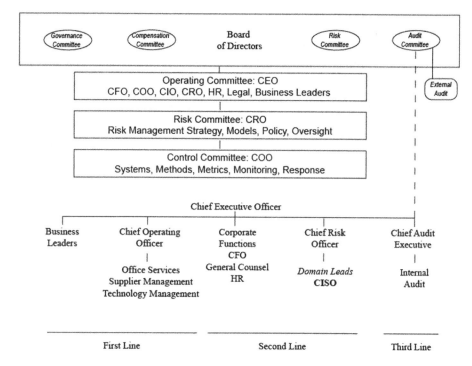

Figure 6-1. *Example of a governance operating model*

Regardless of whether the formal OCC-recommended "three lines of defense" approach is adopted, a key control embedded in the model is independent reporting lines from the level below a financial institution's CEO throughout risk management functions. The horizontal lines at the bottom of Figure 6-1 label the numeric "line" of the management members listed above them. Business executives should ideally establish complete and comprehensive risk and control practices within "first line" management. Risk managers in other corporate functions should monitor the first line activity using risk appetite statements and associated risk tolerance metrics. These metrics should be developed in collaboration with first line management to ensure transparency. These "second line" individuals also qualify as management and monitor policy compliance, but they do not actively manage financial services or operations. Yet, as "second line" managers their observations are inherently more objective than those first line managers who build and run business services. The second line relies upon a shared ERM framework and individual policy domains to properly interpret first line activities and metrics. The third line is "internal audit." They audit both the efficacy of the risk management practices and their proper application by both the first and second line. "External audit" is independent even of the CEO and also opines on the efficacy of internal audit. The BoD leverages the independent opinions of both internal and external auditors to gain assurance that the information they receive is both accurate and comprehensive.

Note that the committees referenced in Figure 6-1 typically include members from across the three lines of defense, although the chair is usually the executive with primary responsibility for the committee's reports to the BoD. The committees are designed to ensure that risks are raised to an appropriate level of senior management so action may be promptly taken. The CEO is responsible for creating the business organizational structure that allows the cross-fertilization of ideas and experiences throughout all lines of defense. Second line management is primarily responsible for making sure all relevant risks are identified and properly referred to those accountable for implementing controls to minimize risks to an acceptable residual level. Third line management is primarily responsible for independent risk assessment and risk escalation. It is critically important that all three lines of defense agree on the information used to represent business processes, controls, and risks. These governance committees provide forums to share such "ground truth."

Committees will typically document management intent with respect to their scope of responsibilities in a charter. They typically issue firm-wide policy with respect to the domain of their primary responsibility and define and record activities with respect to governance of that policy. These may include setting roles and responsibilities, defining risk appetite, establishing standards for implementation, and/or mandatory use of tools, techniques, or procedures for accomplishing tasks within the scope of the governance responsibilities. Committee meetings are also used for strategy setting, communicating with stakeholders, and monitoring performance. Figure 6-1 depicts a corporate structure wherein three key committees direct and oversee corporate functions, but committee structure varies widely across organizations. However, it is common for members to overlap and for agenda topics to be welcome from members of management who may not be committee members.

Leaders must keep in mind that these committees, and the records they keep, actually do represent "ground truth" when it comes to risk management. Without the rigor provided by such a formal structure, management accountability fades into a cloud of plausible deniability. If it appears to staff that there is an alternative or *shadow* governance structure where decisions are *really* made outside of the oversight of these committees, disrespect for the governance activities will ferment and critical issues will escape attention. This is why so often in discussions on governance there is a critical emphasis on *culture*. It is also why risk management at the enterprise level begins with understanding the dimensions of strategy-mission, vision, and core values of the organization. Any contribution of governance to strategy can occur only when they are approached in *lock step*.

The words "lock step" suggest synchronization, rather than a somewhat weaker term that is often used to emphasize governance and leadership strategy must be in sync, that is: *alignment*. "Alignment" evokes an image of independent drivers on parallel tracks, frequently glancing at each other to prevent getting too far apart. "Lock step" instead offers an image of groups marching together to the same drumbeat, momentum building on the trust that the collective team is going in the right direction. If a leader is uncomfortable with the mechanisms that drive committee structure, finds the communications capabilities weak, or has some other gripe with committee efficiency or effectiveness, then the committee culture should evolve to accommodate leadership rather than the other way around.

However it may be implemented, the goal of governance is to provide accountability for creating building blocks by which sound management is put into effect: organizational structures, policies, resource allocation, standards, and procedures. From the building blocks of accountability and management direction come processes and technologies that are complementary and combine to ensure that governance objectives are achieved and may be monitored. For example, in the context of work on an operating committee, a human resources function may be charged with maintaining an employee "code of conduct" that is supported by a wide variety of other committee member organizations and is used by everyone in the firm. In a code of conduct, there will typically be a list of policies issued by all committees and attestation that employees will comply with all policies. Although the code itself is just one policy in the overall financial institution's governance operating model, it provides a great example of how the committees need to work together on strategy to achieve mutual objectives and is one reason why human resources is a significant player in any governance operating model.

In Figure 6-1, the Chief Information Security Officer (CISO) is shown as a "domain lead." Though other domain leads are not shown due to space constraints, the CISO would be expected to have counterparts in credit, market, operational, and other risk domains. As such, the person in the role may be expected to author a "cybersecurity policy" for review and adoption by the risk committee. The assignment of the CISO to a second line reflects a growing trend to ensure that the CISO's opinion on the adequacy of cybersecurity controls is not tainted by participation in or decision-making with respect to control design. In organizations with fewer domain leads, a cybersecurity policy may instead be incorporated into a broader firm-wide Technology Risk Management or Operational Risk Management policy. Regardless of its author, there should be at least one firm-wide policy that clearly defines management's intent with respect to cybersecurity risk, and it should clearly be part of the enterprise governance structure.

Cybersecurity Risk Appetite

The manner by which committees move policy from paper exercises to functioning risk management activities can vary widely. Nevertheless, there are common components to ERM that are consistent not only across the financial industry but across any firm sizable enough to have established a formal risk management program. The key to effective design and implementation of a cybersecurity risk management program is to recognize these components at a high level and to leverage the strengths of the organization in their service. As described by the Committee of Sponsoring Organizations of the Treadway Commission (COSO), ERM is a principle-based framework designed to provide reasonable expectation that the organization understands and manages risks associated with strategy and business objectives, and these principles are grouped into five basic components:[4]

1. Governance & Culture

2. Strategy & Objective-Setting

3. Performance

4. Review & Revision

5. Information, Communication, & Reporting

Figure 6-2 summarizes the principles by component. As COSO itself is comprised of major financial accounting and audit associations whose members actively participate in publishing activities, and also maintains standards on internal control, the COSO ERM Framework provides a strong foundation for integrating the management of all types of risk. Cybersecurity risk is no exception.

Governance & culture	Performance
1. Exercises board risk oversight	10. Identifies risk
2. Establishes operating structures	11. Assesses severity of risk
3. Defines desired culture	12. Prioritizes risks
4. Demonstrates commitment to core values	13. Implements risk responses
	14. Develops portfolio view
5. Attracts, develops, and retains capable individuals	
Strategy & objective-setting	**Review & revision**
6. Analyzes business context	15. Assesses substantial change
7. Defines risk appetite	16. Reviews risk and performance
8. Evaluates alternative strategies	17. Pursues improvement in enterprise risk management
9. Formulates business objectives	
Information, communication, and reporting	
18. Leverages information systems	
19. Communicates risk information	
20. Reports on risk, culture, and performance	

Figure 6-2. *COSO ERM principles*

Just as enterprise mission and vision are foundational to the development of strategic plans, strategic plans themselves require a foundation of governance elements, performance measurement, and internal control. Risk managers in all fields weigh the probability that activities prompted by a given strategy may result in foreseeable future events that will have a negative impact on mission. They also assess the integrity of the planned governance structures, the suitability of the performance measures, and the strength of the internal controls. This is an ongoing process and relies heavily on the establishment of appropriate governance structures, as the primary method of identifying and averting these events is to use established governance structures to assist in framing decisions.

Note that although the COSO ERM Framework principles are numbered, there is no prescribed sequential order for the risk management activities. Like cybersecurity loops (i.e., identify-protect-detect-respond-recover), all components are expected to run simultaneously and support each other in the service of cybersecurity risk management. However, it is important to understand ERM Framework components are expected to reflect an enterprise level perspective so they can be leveraged for broad cybersecurity risk management goals, not created specifically to support specific objectives. Particularly in the cases of *Governance*, *Strategy*, and *Reporting*, cybersecurity risks managed independently of ERM are not likely to gain sufficient support from management strategy, nor can they be appropriately escalated.

To manage cybersecurity risk, it is appropriate first to verify that the governance and culture elements of the ERM Framework incorporate both technology risk and cybersecurity risk in a straightforward manner. BoD oversight and operating structures necessary for integrating cybersecurity risk assessment into strategic planning is key. The definition of cybersecurity risk appetite should be well-understood and codified in a manner that binds the entire organization to consider it when making strategic plans in any endeavor. That said, as yet very few financial institutions have a formal Cybersecurity Risk Program. The 2017 PWC Risk in Review study reported that, while 55 percent of respondents reported that risk appetite or tolerance has been defined across a number of key risk categories, only 9 percent reported the maturity level of their cybersecurity risk program was high or very high, and 76 percent reported that it was low or very low.[5] A follow-up study in 2018 revealed that only 27% of companies say they are "very comfortable" the board is getting adequate reporting on metrics on cyber and privacy risk management.[6] Unfortunately, this suggests that although there are occasionally speculative articles on what cybersecurity risk appetite might look like,[7] at the time of this publication there are no authoritative examples in the literature on financial services cybersecurity risk appetite statements. The OCC itself has published its Enterprise Risk Appetite Statement and does not have a separate category for cybersecurity risk, though it does mention the risk of unauthorized access in a more general statement on Technology Risk Appetite.[8] Nevertheless, the OCC publication does afford a look at what an industry standard Risk Appetite Statement related to technology or security looks like. It appears in Figure 6-3.

> The OCC's appetite for technology risk is low. Information systems must support core agency functions with sufficient capability, capacity, resiliency, and security from internal and external threats. The agency relies on an increasingly mobile and technologically dependent workforce to carry out its core mission. Therefore, the OCC has a low appetite for unreliable technology. The OCC will ensure a robust technological infrastructure that meets its workforce and operational needs while supporting measured innovation.
>
> - The OCC has no appetite for unauthorized access to systems and confidential data and will maintain strong controls to mitigate external threats against its technology infrastructure.
> - The OCC has a low appetite for losing continuity of business operations stemming from unreliable telecommunications or system availability. Business resiliency planning and execution must be aligned with strategic objectives.
> - The OCC has a moderate appetite for innovative technology solutions to meet user demands in a rapidly changing environment. The agency will exercise appropriate governance and discipline when considering and adopting new technology.

Figure 6-3. *OCC Technology Risk Appetite Statement*

It is easy to extrapolate from the example in Figure 6-3 that a cybersecurity-specific Risk Appetite Statement should be structured as something like the paragraph in Figure 6-4.

> All financial products rely on digital technology to connect customers to services for deposit, payments, savings, investment, and insurance. The firm continuously innovates and improves technologies to facilitate identification, authentication, authorization, integrity, and availability of these financial services. Therefore, the Firm has no appetite for Cybersecurity Risks that negatively impact customer privacy, the integrity of financial records, and/or facilitate the unauthorized transfer of ownership of financial assets. Due to inherent risks in maintaining an adequate pace of change, the firm has a low tolerance for disruptions in availability of financial services.

Figure 6-4. *Example cybersecurity Risk Appetite Statement*

After risk appetite has been qualitatively determined, the challenge shifts from definition to measurement. Risk appetite broadly describes the amount of risk a firm is willing to accept, it is also important to differentiate this from risk capacity, or the maximum amount of risk the firm is able to absorb. The relationship between risk appetite and risk capacity allows analysis with which to compare alternative strategies to support management decision-making. At this level of discussion, risk can seem like a vague term. Risk refers to an aggregate view of potential negative events in whatever category that modifies the term (e.g., market risk, credit risk, or cybersecurity risk). But risks in plural refer to the possibility that discrete events within the category will occur and affect the achievement of strategy and business objectives. Attempts to measure conformance to risk appetite highlights attributes of actual risks and reveals the units with which risk appetite and risk capacity are measured within a risk category. Most risk categories are measured in currency, the money lost when a risk event occurs. In cybersecurity risk, money is the primary unit of measurement only in fraud cases. In other cases, it could be customers lost, reputational damage, systems downtime, or interruption in critical services. All of these variables relate to performance against business objectives. Risk appetite needs to stay below risk capacity. Risk tolerance refers to the range of degraded performance that management deems acceptable.

The terms "risk tolerance measures" and "key risk indicators" are sometimes used interchangeably. However, risk tolerance measures refer specifically to the boundaries of acceptable variations in performance related to achieving objectives, while risk indicators are measures that help identify changes to the risks themselves. An example of a key risk indicator unrelated to performance is the Index of Cybersecurity, a monthly survey of cybersecurity professionals that crowd-sources perceptions of cybersecurity risk and compiles an index on a monthly basis. Figure 6-5 is an excerpt from that organization's monthly report, which shows the risks that are perceived by cybersecurity professionals to have risen most dramatically in the past month. The Index of Cybersecurity is also a good example of an independent and external key risk indicator. For another example, if there were news reports in the *Wall Street Journal* that banks using internet-facing software similar to the firm had experienced cybersecurity breaches, it would be an undeniable key risk indicator that an event in which the firm may experience damage has become more likely. There are also multiple vendor services that will scour the web for cybersecurity risks specific to a given company, or the financial services industry. Such externally generated key risk indicators should be consulted to ensure that the set of risks in the cybersecurity risk category is as complete as possible.

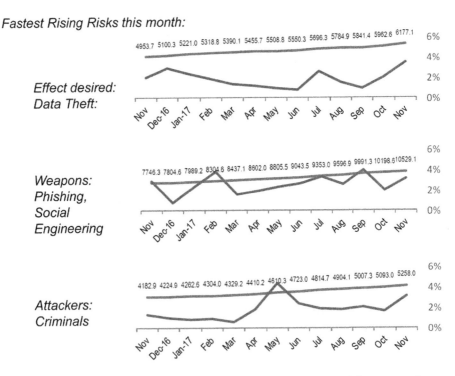

***Figure 6-5.** Excerpt from Index of Cybersecurity Monthly Report[9]*

Figure 6-6 is an example of risk tolerance monitoring mechanisms applied to the business objectives referred to in the Risk Appetite Statement in Figure 6-4. The risk appetite for events that impact the first set of business objectives is lower (no tolerance) than the business objective on the availability of services (low tolerance). Figure 6-6(a) shows risk appetite as zero, and tolerance measures that over time recorded one breach of risk appetite. Figure 6-6(b) shows measures of tolerance that stay within risk appetite but are trending higher. Figure 6-6(b) also shows a situation where a risk tolerance measure may also be a key risk indicator and overlaps with a performance indicator. The risk appetite with respect to service availability would presumably be measured with service performance attributes, and it makes sense to use negative trends in service performance as a key risk indicator. Other performance measures may also be risk indicators but not key risk indicators—for example, staff attrition in a robust but stable job market.

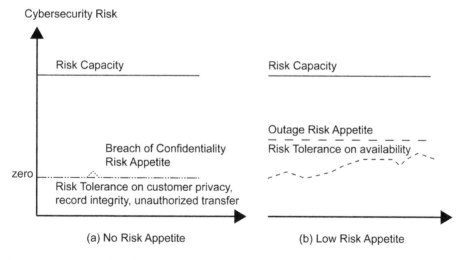

Figure 6-6. *Risk tolerance monitoring*

Alternative strategies for defining each of the qualitative elements of risk appetite should be evaluated to ensure they are in lock-step with business objectives for financial service provisioning and maintenance. The definitions will dictate business and technology quantitative measures that reinforce the risk appetite definitions with specific goals. Variation in the achievement of the goals should be defined as risk tolerance measures. Many of those goals will relate to technology control performance measures, and it should be clear when performance measures indicate that risk appetite has been breached. As business objectives are formulated from a financial product perspective and technology roadmap perspective, these risk tolerance measures should also evolve to ensure their connection to risk appetite remains valid.

Cybersecurity Performance Objectives

Risk appetite reflects the organization's overall posture with respect to taking on various levels of risk. In practice, however, an exemplar performance objective is needed to translate the appetite into action, and thereby maintain secure system configuration. In order to achieve that objective, multiple control objectives must be operating simultaneously, and each will have measures that indicate whether the performance objective is met. Figure 6-7 depicts a typical financial systems architecture.

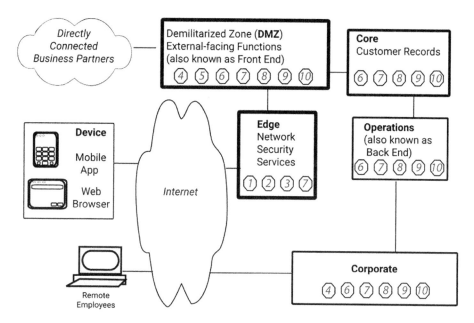

Figure 6-7. *Example financial service network, cybersecurity controls enumerated*

Performance measures over configuration within the architecture include, but are not limited to:

1. Domain name configuration

2. Load balancing targets

3. Denial of service environment failover test results

4. Public network protocol secure termination

5. Web server configuration, including plug-in modules and data feeds

6. Secure software life cycle

7. Network and operating system configuration, process monitoring and automated response to anomalies

8. User group membership synchronization with job function and task assignments

9. Network, operating system, and application activity log monitoring, alerting, and measured time to respond

10. Independent software control review—code review results, white box penetration test results

Each of the measures records some aspects of performance, but the "secure configuration" performance objective is not met unless the data shows that all aspects of systems configuration are operating as expected. However, it is unreasonable to expect continuous, near-perfect performance in all aspects, and disruptions in operations may have substantial downstream impact. Some minimal deviations in performance measures must be tolerated, although this does not necessarily mean risk is increased. While it is possible that some performance measures are also key risk indicators, it is also true that many controls are redundant, so to declare a performance indicator a key risk indicator, there needs to be some rationale that a dip in a typically robust performance measure actually increases the probability that an adversary will be able to exploit it to produce a negatively impacting event. To determine the sets of controls most effective at reducing risk (sometimes referred to as key controls) the inherent risk of successful cyber attack should be compared to the risk that exists after controls have been established. In a situation where none of the controls in Figure 6-7 are implemented, the probability a web server will be compromised is intolerably high. In a situation where they are all functioning effectively, the probability is drastically reduced. In a situation where only controls 1, 2, and 3 are implemented, it is still highly probable that an attack will be successful. However, if instead only controls 4, 5, and 6 are implemented, the probability of a successful attack is dramatically reduced in comparison with the previous case. This type of probability measure is called *residual* risk, the risk that remains after controls have been established. Performance targets with respect to cybersecurity are all intended to widen the gap between inherent and residual risk.

Performance is a term used broadly and sometimes too generally. Performance can be used with respect to proceeding toward business objectives but also refers to the observed (or perceived) effectiveness of implemented controls. In the ERM view of Figure 6-2, performance refers to the ERM process itself, which we can say is performing well when it is able to identify, assess, and prioritize risk, implement controls, and develop a portfolio view of the risks that remain.

As in any other risk domain, responsibility for managing cybersecurity risk is typically the responsibility of the first line. Risk management activity includes both the establishment of an information security program and a connection between the controls established by the program and the risks it is meant to reduce. Once this connection has been made, building artifacts like the diagram in Figure 6-7 in a risk assessment process, the Information Security Program itself may be used to represent ground truth. The progression from risk assessment to security policy construction, policy implementation, policy compliance, and policy monitoring has been routine for cybersecurity professionals for decades. A recent survey of cybersecurity management professionals affirmed that these connections are key and further that both management and employee support are critical to success.[10] When these links are firmly established, verification that risks are managed becomes synonymous with the breakdown of information security program elements into attributes that may be independently verified.

Regulatory rules and commonly followed financial industry information security policies provide well-recognized examples of cybersecurity risk management activity. As an example, consider the US Gramm-Leach-Bliley Act (GLBA). GLBA requires that financial institutions ensure the security and confidentiality of personally identifiable financial information. A subset of the regulation intended to support the enforcement of GLBA is the Federal Trade Commission (FTC) Safeguards Rule that requires financial institutions to have measures in place to keep customer information secure.[11] These requirements reflect common sense goals of data protection from the perspective of financial industry business practice, therefore representing good internal policy. Figure 6-8 highlights 16 CFR 314, Standards for Safeguarding Customer Information, guidance that provides an excellent basis for cybersecurity governance.

§ 314.4 Elements.
In order to develop, implement, and maintain your information security program, you shall:

(a) Designate an employee or employees to coordinate your information security program.

(b) Identify reasonably foreseeable internal and external risks to the security, confidentiality, and integrity of customer information that could result in the unauthorized disclosure, misuse, alteration, destruction or other compromise of such information, and assess the sufficiency of any safeguards in place to control these risks. At a minimum, such a risk assessment should include consideration of risks in each relevant area of your operations, including:

(1) Employee training and management;

(2) Information systems, including network and software design, as well as information processing, storage, transmission and disposal; and

(3) Detecting, preventing and responding to attacks, intrusions, or other systems failures.

(c) Design and implement information safeguards to control the risks you identify through risk assessment, and regularly test or otherwise monitor the effectiveness of the safeguards' key controls, systems, and procedures.

(d) Oversee service providers, by:

(1) Taking reasonable steps to select and retain service providers that are capable of maintaining appropriate safeguards for the customer information at issue; and

(2) Requiring your service providers by contract to implement and maintain such safeguards.

(e) Evaluate and adjust your information security program in light of the results of the testing and monitoring required by paragraph (c) of this section; any material changes to your operations or business arrangements; or any other circumstances that you know or have reason to know may have a material impact on your information security program.

Figure 6-8. Example requirement: GLBA's FTC Safeguards Rule[12]

A cybersecurity governance group would of course be expected to have an information security program in place and would of course be expected to formally compare its program to the requirements listed in the regulatory rule. Figure 6-9 is an example table of contents of a financial institution's information security management program shown side by side with an abbreviated version of the elements of the FTC Safeguard Rule.

FTC Safeguards Rule Elements	Information Security Program Elements
(a) Designate an employee or employees to coordinate your information security program. (b) Identify reasonably foreseeable internal and external risks to customer information. (c) Design and implement information safeguards (d) Oversee service providers (e) Evaluate and adjust your information security program in light of the results of the testing and monitoring.	1. Information Security Management 2. Information Classification 3. Cybersecurity Risk Appetite 4. Information Security Policy 5. Technology Control Standards 6. Cybersecurity Risk Assessment 7. Risk Issue Identification & Treatment 8. Cybersecurity Support Processes

Figure 6-9. *Comparison of GLBA's FTC Safeguards Rule with an information security program*

Effective governance can be demonstrated in part by comparing to regulation or a corporate framework. We say "in part" as there is more to governance than adhering to standards or regulatory objectives. What typically occurs is that a risk analyst will decompose a regulation into list of control requirements. Components of the internal control framework are then "mapped" onto a regulation. The decomposition and mapping demonstrates that a regulation may be covered via the internal control framework requirement and associated monitoring process. To many people new to cybersecurity governance roles, it can appear that all there is to showing compliance with regulations is to show how internal documents such as the information security program table of contents map to the regulation, as in the example in Figure 6-10. Of course, there should be a deeper level of detail in the mapping where the actual internal security program control objective, or a combination of several, would be excerpted and displayed rather than merely indicated, as in the example of Figure 6-10. Nevertheless, the figure is illustrative of any such mapping. Comparing policy to regulatory rules only demonstrates compliance if the evidence of compliance with internal policy also is suitable evidence of compliance with the rule.

	A. Designate a coordinator for Information Security Program	B. Identify Internal and External Risks	C. Design and Implement Information Safeguards	D. Oversee Service Providers	E. Continuous Monitoring and Adjustment of Info Security Program
1. Information Security Management Overview	✓				✓
2. Information Classification		✓			
3. Cybersecurity Risk Appetite		✓			
4. Information Security Policy		✓	✓	✓	
5. Technology Control Standards		✓	✓	✓	
6. Cybersecurity Risk Assessment		✓		✓	✓
7. Risk Issue Identification & Treatment		✓			✓
8. Cybersecurity Support Processes		✓	✓		

Figure 6-10. *Level map from GLBA's FTC Safeguards Rule to a security program*

Consider the mapping derived from Figure 6-10 would essentially be a theory of compliance based on a claim of equivalence between the regulation and the internal controls described in the information security program. Logically, it may be represented as a proof based on inference. Continuing the example, assume that the first few sections of the security program outlined in Figure 6-10 are documented in Figure 6-11. Note the bold and italicized statements in each section of the program in Figure 6-11 correspond to the mapped cells in Figure 6-10 (i.e., [<FTC Column><Security Program Row>]), and therefore supply proof the internal framework complies with the FTC Safeguards Rule. This logical equivalence holds even though the information security policy does not require businesses to use the information classification levels that would trigger the technology controls standards for appropriate safeguards. Instead, it requires risk identification, not treatment, for customer information and where information is provided to third parties, it refers vaguely to "sensitive information," and leaves that treatment entirely to the business.

1. Information Security Management Overview

The **employee designated to coordinate our information Security Program is the Chief Information Security Officer [A, 1].**

The Chief Information Security Officer must **evaluate and adjust information security [E,1]** as needed to maintain Cybersecurity within Risk Appetite.

2. Information Classification

Information classification levels "Public", "Internal", "Customer Confidential", and "Restricted" are established to facilitate **the identification of reasonably foreseeable internal and external risks to the security, confidentiality, and integrity of customer information [B.2].**

3. Cybersecurity Risk Appetite

The Chief Information Security Officer must **establish Cybersecurity Risk Appetite [B,3]** for the firm that specifically refers to information by classification level.

4. Information Security Policy

Business data owners must **identify reasonably foreseeable internal and external risks to the security, confidentiality, and integrity of customer information [B,4].**

Businesses who engage third parties with access to sensitive information must **oversee service providers [D,4]** to ensure information security policy requirements and technology control standards are upheld.

5. Technology Control Standards

Technology operations must **design and implement information safeguards [C,4]** that appropriately protect information at each information classification level.

Etc.

Figure 6-11. *Example security program that logically complies with FTC Safeguards Rule*

Regardless of whether a regulatory rule is evaluated directly or with respect to an internal framework, any actual proof of a logical statement such as that in Figure 6-11 should involve not only a documented comparison but also a technology inventory, observations, comparisons, and conclusions. Most institutions struggle to demonstrate that rules within internal frameworks are actually followed, and therefore governance teams should avoid assumptions without actual evidence of implementation. For example, a strategy may include performance measures that require help desk services to resolve customer or employee onboarding issues within a minimal period of time. If the stated timeframe is not adequate to verify the user's identity, then the strategy may present an unacceptable level of cybersecurity risk.

It is imperative that cybersecurity governance has access to a readily available, enterprise-wide technology and information inventory that corresponds to business process and data content. The inventory should be used to collect observations and metrics that demonstrate controls are in place, and those observations and metrics should be used to demonstrate compliance with both regulatory and business control requirements. Where policies and standards help facilitate this demonstration, this makes the job easier. But the policies and standards themselves cannot substitute for it. Ideally, the security program creates the rationales that allow conclusions that rules are followed and helps identify risk issues that may or may not lead to changes in technology or governance process. Where changes are warranted, the governance function is primarily responsible for ensuring budgets are allocated and projects are initiated. Although the projects and changes in operation of cybersecurity controls are usually performed in engineering or development groups, the governance function oversees those remediation activities to provide management with assurance that timelines are appropriate to ensure risks are reduced as soon as practicable, and that milestones are monitored so potential failures in control improvements are quickly identified, escalated, and rectified.

It is important to emphasize to teams that may potentially be assigned to governance roles that such mapping exercises should always start with business process, and the scope of compliance demonstration should flow top-down, from accurate representation of business process flows that include reference to all information within the scope of a rule. That is, the information flow required by any technology-related governance process is the same as that required by any audit or assessment of technology. They must start with a complete list of relevant processes within the scope of a given rule, identify the technology controls and evidence that indicates if they are in place, and seek to determine whether they actually operate in accordance with the rules delineated in the internal framework. Figure 6-12 outlines the steps that governance processes generally follow in any technology compliance assessment. The difference in a governance role is that all rules must be evaluated continuously and simultaneously. Only then can the assumptions in Figure 6-10 be well-founded.

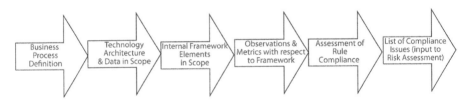

Figure 6-12. *Cybersecurity assessment strategy data flow*

Demonstration that a rule is followed should always include not only the combination of the policies, procedures, assignments of roles, and responsibilities for implementation and maintenance, but also metrics used for reporting to the committees responsible for oversight. For example, the FTC Safeguards Rule requires identification of all business processes that handle customers' personally identifiable information. That is typically available via an operational risk management system (ORM) in a process table. That system may have a listing of applications that is associated with the process and will be identified via an index from an application inventory system. The application inventory can typically be queried to identify the technology platforms that compose the application. A configuration management database (CMDB) may then be queried using the application index to identify the infrastructure equipment used to support a given application. The network configuration of the infrastructure may then be queried to determine how data flows into and out of the application. Each type of technology component identified in these exercises may have a history of audits and assessments, projects, change management records, incident and problem management records. These may be used to gain assurance (or not) that internal framework rules are observed. Most of the safeguard requirements pertaining to cybersecurity should be visible to the governance team via these types of metrics and therefore can inform the discussion of them within committees. If a complete picture cannot be painted, the team may use the gap to justify the development of new metrics. Members of the cybersecurity governance group will also typically use these forums to communicate new and evolving risk issues as well as gain consensus on risk prioritization and risk reductions plans.

Action item registers and meeting minutes of committee discussions serve as first and second line due diligence to record the reporting of and response to errors or gaps in implementation of controls. Although the third line attends these committees, their oversight evidence is typically confined to formal audit reports and summaries of these reports to the Audit Committee of the BoD. These formal reports, in combination with day-to-day management oversight activities, such as weekly project status meetings and production change management committees, provide ample data to allow a governance function to see whether or not implemented controls support a case for internal framework compliance. If this is the case, then regulatory compliance demonstrations may rely on logic such as that in Figure 6-10. Otherwise, the business process must be revisited with each new regulatory requirement, and full analysis performed as referenced by Figure 6-12. That is, even if all the evidence were completely verified for internal control rules, final assessment of regulatory rule compliance should include a documented rationale to support the assumptions that (1) if the rule is followed, compliance will result, and (2) the rule is followed.

Cybersecurity governance thus relies on a strong foundation of technology inventory, secure architecture, and configuration standards. It typically relies upon frequent data feeds from application and infrastructure inventories, configuration management databases, project management systems, change management, and incident management systems into governance, risk and control (GRC) systems. It is not important for the cybersecurity governance function to own the data repositories, but it should have continuous access to them in order to monitor and assess systems' compliance with both internal and external frameworks. That is, the data feeds into the GRC system may be high-level summaries or metrics that may indicate potential issues, and the governance staff should be able to login to the source systems to examine details underlying summaries and metrics. Figure 6-13 lists some of the metrics mentioned here and other types of data repositories that are typically useful for cybersecurity governance.

Repository	Useful Data
Anti-malware	History of attempts and intrusions on both user desktops and servers.
Application Inventory	Records of technology that has an authorized business purpose.
Regulatory Compliance	List of which regulations correspond to which businesses.
Change Management	History of changes to applications and infrastructure, statistics on change delays, failures, and corresponding incidents.
Cybersecurity Threat	Current threat analysis for software and infrastructure platforms.
Email, Messaging, & File Transfer	Capabilities for content management and data loss prevention.
Identity & Access Management	All active system users and entitlements corresponding to authorized job functions (or not).
Governance, Risk, and Control	Information security policy, process, and procedures, typically supplemented with metrics extracted from other systems.
Key Management	Type and frequency of encryption in use by platform and/or application.
Network Data Flow	Ports and network traffic filters configured on servers and in network switches, routers, and firewalls.
Operating System Security	Compliance with standard platform builds for both operating systems and platform stack software and middleware.
Operational Risk Management	Business process flows, cybersecurity risk assessment results, process-to-application mapping, and cybersecurity risk scenario analysis results.
Penetration Tests	The set of vulnerabilities tested corresponds to current threat analysis results.
Problem & Incident Management	Technology operational support issues, assignments and members of support personal and application development means, problem root cause analysis.
Program & Project Management	Budgets, projects, timelines, milestones and project status.
Security Incidents	Records demonstrating compliance with response procedure.
Storage Management	Compliance with security standards for unstructured data.

Figure 6-13. *Cybersecurity governance metrics sources*

153

Without a strong understanding of the enterprise risk structure on the part of cybersecurity governance, and ownership of the integrity of the data in the repositories, the metrics by which compliance is demonstrated will be highly suspect and is likely to be discredited by both non-technical auditors as well as technical penetration testers.

Moving Ahead

This chapter examined considerations in managing the cybersecurity controls architecture. This includes operationalizing various risk treatment decisions such as new technology adoption and the development of supporting processes. However, it also must include establishing sound governance to support effective management oversight of the continuous pace of changes to internal organizational architectures and processes, as well as external drivers such as shifting threat dimensions and evolving regulatory frameworks. If not closely managed, the cybersecurity controls architecture can expand management's intended boundaries, drawing in substantial resources. The next chapter explores the concern that, if not adequately managed, cybersecurity activities can inefficiently consume resources across the enterprise.

Notes

1. Drucker, Peter. *The Essential Drucker*, (New York: HarperCollins, 2001).

2. Deming. W. E., W. The New Economics, *Massachusetts Institute of Technology Press*, 1993, p. 35.

3. OCC Guidelines Establishing Heightened Standards for Certain Large Insured National Banks, Insured Federal Savings Associations, and Insured Federal Branches; Integration of Regulations; Final Rule, *Federal Register*, Volume 79, Issue 176, September 11, 2014.

4. COSO (2017). Enterprise Risk Management: Integrating with Strategy and Performance, Committee of Sponsoring Organizations of the Treadway Commission, Members include: American Accounting Association, American Institute of Certified Public Accountants, Financial Executive Institute, Institute of Internal Auditors, Institute of Management Accountants. This document was originally published in 2004, and updated in 2017. Note, the companion Internal Control document was originally published in 1992, and most recently updated in 2013. See www.coso.org.

5. PWC, 2017, Risk in Review, Managing from the Front Line, https://www.pwc.com/us/en/risk-assurance/risk-in-review-study.html.

6. PwC (2018). The Journey to Digital Trust.pwc.com/us/digitaltrustinsights.

7. Pareek, M. (2013). "What Is Your Risk Appetite?" *ISACA Journal* 4.

8. OCC (2016). Enterprise Risk Appetite Statement. See: https://www.occ.gov/publications/publications-by-type/other-publications-reports/risk-appetite-statement.pdf

9. Geer, D., and Mukul Pareek, *The Index of Cybersecurity*, November, 2017, http://cybersecurityindex.org/

10. Flowerday, S. a. T. T. (2016). "Information Policy Development and Implementation." *Computers & Security* 61: 169-183.

11. Standards for Safeguarding Customer Information; Final Rule - 16 CFR Part 314 (May 23, 2002), *Federal Register* Volume 67 Number 100.

12. 16 CFR Part 314- Standards for Safeguarding Customer Information. https://www.law.cornell.edu/cfr/text/16/part-314

CHAPTER 7

Should This Involve the Whole Organization?

Throughout the past decade we have seen a variety of management experiments with new cybersecurity organizational structures. Many of these were formed hastily in response to management recognizing they were vulnerable to threats, and then grew to fulfill their mission of threat preparedness independently of both business and technology development. Even when cybersecurity departments are part of a technology group, they are often placed under an infrastructure manager and often have not been well-integrated with software specifications or deployments. Instead they focused on assessment and remediation of production environments. Overall, growth in cybersecurity organizations has been somewhat consistent, with Chief Information Security Officers (CISOs) designing enterprise-wide cybersecurity risk programs, piloting security technologies within the technology organization, and then seeking integration touch-points with other organizations as threats became more obvious and ubiquitous. Consequently, many cybersecurity officers have limited visibility into business requirements for technology and as a result may be assumed by their peers to have low levels of

© Paul Rohmeyer, Jennifer L. Bayuk 2019
P. Rohmeyer and J. L. Bayuk, *Financial Cybersecurity Risk Management*,
https://doi.org/10.1007/978-1-4842-4194-3_7

business insight and corresponding contribution to mission.[1] The recent drive to build enterprise capabilities for managing cybersecurity risk represents a change to a more aligned approach wherein cybersecurity is viewed not only as a key consideration in enterprise risk management (ERM) but a key attribute of enterprise architecture.

Architectural View

FDIC's definition of enterprise architecture (EA) is applicable to financial institutions—that is: *a discipline for proactively and holistically leading enterprise responses to disruptive forces by identifying and analyzing the execution of change toward desired business vision and outcomes. EA delivers value by presenting business and IT leaders with signature-ready recommendations for adjusting policies and projects to achieve target business outcomes that capitalize on relevant business disruptions.*[2]

The FFIEC guidance for regulated entities, in the FFIEC IT Examination Handbook, tailored this definition for IT as:

Enterprise architecture (EA) is the overall design and high-level plan that describes an institution's operational framework and includes the institution's mission, stakeholders, business and customers, work flow and processes, data processing, access, security, and availability.[3]

The guidance repeatedly refers to security when listing considerations for technology management with respect to EA. For example:

Key considerations when developing an EA program include security, business resilience, data management, external connectivity, and alignment with the institution's goals and objectives. To effectively implement an EA program, the institution should analyze the risks and potential impact of threats to all of the institution's activities. A comprehensive EA program based on prudent practices can help an institution better develop processes to manage IT issues and identify, measure, and mitigate technology-based risks and threats.[4]

Although financial services management has routinely followed the COSO Internal Control mandate for support via tone-at-the-top, the management approach to cybersecurity does not generally utilize a comprehensive top-down, enterprise-wide view of enterprise architecture. Rather, technology roles and responsibilities are typically set top-down, and each business unit is free to design systems in accordance with their unique business requirements. This situation does not reflect on the quality of past technology control standards issued by governance organizations such as ISACA, ISO, or NIST. These standards have long recommended cybersecurity risk be considered at the highest levels of strategic planning and have consistently recommended the integration approach should be holistic and top-down. Figure 7-1 illustrates the relationship between governance and management as recommended by COSO and COBIT standards. It is clearly the role of governance to ensure risk optimization for all risk categories, including cybersecurity. Governance is meant to ensure that management performs risk assessment in strategy selection, aligns operations with risk management activities, and facilitates adequate risk monitoring and oversight. This is an EA approach. Figure 7-1 illustrates the approach typically found in EA literature.

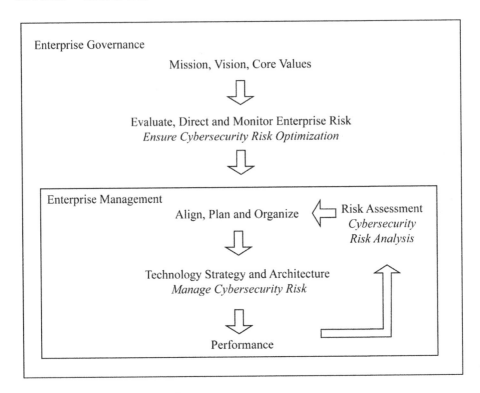

Figure 7-1. *EA approach*

Alignment with EA should ideally start with establishing, or documenting, a vision of the enterprise architecture. The architecture perspective popularized by the Zachman *Framework for Information Systems Architecture* provides a useful mechanism to illustrate enterprise architecture.[5] The idea started as a method to use analogies to building architecture to describe information systems. Zachman metaphorically copied the sequential deliverables of building architects, from intuitive sketches to scale drawings to engineering plans, and created a framework for representing information systems at each successive level of detail. Using those concepts allowed the technologist to create a descriptive framework from disciplines quite independent of information systems, by using analogies to specify systems architecture. Analogy was then used to demonstrate that the resulting system fulfills the requirements of the people, organizations, and processes represented in the intuitive sketches. As Zachman put it, "The architect's drawings are a transcription of the owner's perceptual requirements." Subsequent approaches to modeling enterprise architecture can similarly be applied to enable deeper analysis. For example, TOGAF is a suitable framework that incorporates domains of business, application, data, and technology, and each respectively presents unique perspectives to the cybersecurity architect.[6] The specific choice of framework within a given organization may be determined by factors such as the prevailing architectural view. Consistency in architectural perspectives is fundamental to the goal of ensuring cybersecurity is considered part of a given organization's enterprise architecture plans. Without it, there is no yardstick by which the cybersecurity program can be measured.

An abbreviated example of an enterprise framework is presented in Figure 7-2. It shows how mapping systems requirements to business in multiple dimensions can reveal integrated technology and business requirements. Just as in architectural diagrams used for building construction, Zachman-like framework dimensions are isomorphic, and this isomorphism can prove very helpful in understanding the semantic connection linking technology and business contexts. In Figure 7-2, column 1 lists isomorphic dimensions of technology, and the other column headings are questions or techniques used to map the dimensions to enterprise systems architecture components. Each row answers the questions of the respective column headings and the whole is meant to demonstrate how technology supports the business.

DIMENSION	PEOPLE	OBJECTIVE
Context	Executive – Governance	Business Goals
Concept	Product – Strategy	Process Definition
Logical	Technology – Software	Portals, Databases, Platforms
Physical	Technology- Hardware	Devices, Data Centers
Component	Product - Specifications	Payment Processing
Operation	Product - Support	Customer Support Center

Figure 7-2. *"Zachman-Like" framework approach*

Of course, any analogy necessarily carries assumptions on the part of the listener, and the closer the representation gets to the actual technology tools and techniques, the less intuitive it becomes. Such frameworks serve to structure the problem of integrating automated systems into business operations in an intuitive manner. But once the actual system is built, the tendency has been to represent a system in the absence of the context in which it was motivated. There are typically so many overlapping technology components used to support any one business process or operation, any accurate description would probably be too technically complex for executive communication. So instead, technology executives tend to fall back on abstractions in the form of functional block diagrams and implied relationships between them. For example, typical financial industry technology architecture is often presented to executives and BoD members in a format similar to Figure 7-3.

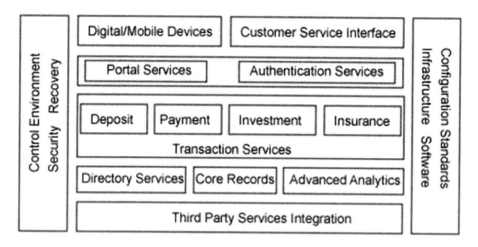

Figure 7-3. *Systems architecture framework*

Although well-intended and potentially useful scaffolding for executive talking points, these diagrams can sometimes be misleading. The conceptual leap in moving from Figure 7-2 to Figure 7-3 cannot be bridged with anything but a thorough education in computer science and several years of experience in financial systems development and infrastructure support. To an executive looking at Figure 7-3, it is not clear how the more abstract boxes like "Portal Services" and "Authentication Services" work, so the reader may make assumptions that business requirements for authentication and authorization are somehow fully met via some interaction with the "Control Environment" box on the left-hand side. By contrast, a technologist experienced in the used of these diagrams would understand the "Control Environment" side-box typically refers only to infrastructure or general controls. Though even a technologist would not know from the diagram anything about how they worked, or what components of the middle columns they covered, or even what technology comprised the components in the middle columns. The depiction of cybersecurity as building blocks in these diagrams is not very helpful where executives are reaching to understand the business context of systems in operation.

Figure 7-4 is a typical C-level/BoD-level diagram depicting how cybersecurity controls integrate with the EA. Note that both the architecture model in Figure 7-2 and the actual systems building blocks in Figure 7-3 have been abstracted away in Figure 7-4. The presentation reads more like a target of an adversary, supplemented with the internal controls that fortify the enterprise against an attacker. The metrics on the right-hand side of the diagram are typically designed to show how each business area is contributing to the control strategy designed by the CISO. Red values indicate breaches in risk tolerance measures; arrows indicate whether the current value represents a positive or negative change from the prior period.

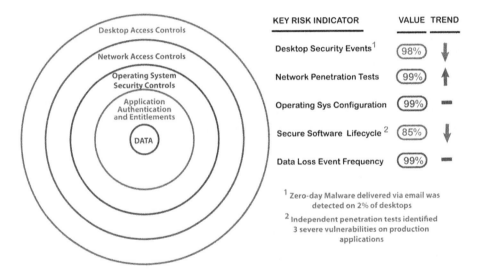

Figure 7-4. *Financial industry cybersecurity BoD presentation*

A presentation such as Figure 7-4 can provide insight into the functioning of the cybersecurity program as it clearly communicates efficacy in control maintenance and an ability to prevent common security incidents. However, it is at best an abstraction from EA to its most common security-related elements, and the technology architecture itself is already abstracted from EA.

This set of examples therefore demonstrates the inadequacy of most technology architecture frameworks as communication vehicles. The translation of financial business concepts to technology is not as straightforward and easily negotiated as the square feet of space in a living room. Technology architecture frameworks serve well to convey decisions made by technology management to those who are expected to standardize components because those subordinates have been part of the decision-making process. They fully comprehend the abstracted details behind the cursory overviews. But technology architecture is not intuitive for non-technical ERM participants, and their interaction with it does not allow them insight into how risks may be identified. As communication with respect to cybersecurity risk is critically dependent on understanding of how technology supports business, it follows we should expect limited understanding of cybersecurity risk at executive and BoD levels.

In theory, diagrams like the one in Figure 7-4 allow a technologist to demonstrate how security control design choices achieve business goals for security. This calls to mind the old adage, "in theory, everything works in practice." In theory, someone has done the business requirements for security and boiled them down into the five sets of controls on the bullseye diagram in Figure 7-4, and in theory, such abstract presentations make perfect sense. In practice, however, the metrics convey very little information with which to intuitively understand cybersecurity risk reduction. Even if they were directly mapped back to the diagram in Figure 7-3, due to the vagueness of that diagram, the explanatory power would still be lacking. Although it may be clear that a single vulnerability, like a webserver authentication gap, can be patched with software, it is not clear why a single vulnerability should expose data, as there is an assumption of multiple layers of control. While some security engineers have called for more detail in Zachman-like approaches to enterprise security architecture,[7] security-specific frameworks frequently introduce more detailed systems attributes that are not business dimensions—for example, security policies, security domains, and security profiles. While these are helpful in communicating to security engineers, in the absence of an actual business process, they do not necessarily make it easier for business to grasp the value of the security constructs.

The lack of clear cybersecurity information in technology presentations has increased the urgency with which executives and BoD members demand presentations on cybersecurity risk. Yet the urgency has not increased the accuracy. In an attempt to facilitate intuitive understanding of information security issues, presentations on "risk" are often designed to convey the severity of the threat and the urgency of budget allocation to address it. Diagrams like that in Figure 7-4 are often accompanied by headline collages such as that in Figure 7-5, and/or metrics showing the business managers who own the technology infrastructure that is not adequately controlled. Information security industry professionals refer to these types of presentations as "scare decks."[8]

Figure 7-5. *Cybersecurity scare factor*

A major consequence of the "scare deck" approach is that, in practice, high-level summaries are often presented to executives and BoD members as sets of technologies that counter threats, in combination with how much the company is spending on the cybersecurity program. As a risk equation, this appears as if capital is allocated to reduce risk. However, there is no real analogy with credit and market risk capital allocation because if there is a cyberattack, the dollars are not a cushion set aside to alleviate the situation. They have been spent on the controls already and may have, in fact, been spent on ineffective controls. Hence, the manner in which cybersecurity dollars translate into enterprise capabilities for cybersecurity should not be the sole decision of the CISO, but a collaborative decision-making process among the best minds in the organization.

Enterprise Capabilities

Much like quality, cybersecurity does not exist in isolation, encapsulated within EA, but impacts throughout the organization. The financial services domain has experienced periodic systemic process improvements in shared financial processing systems and the proliferation of third-party financial software and services. These have created a continuous evolution toward systems interface and data normalization to meet the requirements of integration. The result is an interconnected network of both systemic and ad hoc financial information exchange flowing continuously while changing rapidly. It makes no sense to describe cybersecurity in the absence of the business environment it is meant to protect. It is an integral part of the environment and should be presented and discussed as such; it is not an add-on, bolt-on, or wrapper.

Unfortunately, there are currently no industry standards for the method by which to communicate how cybersecurity is integrated into the enterprise, especially in organizations in which the integration is suspect or failing. There is also virtually no aspect of technology that does not rely on cybersecurity tools and techniques to enable management control. Without cybersecurity, there cannot be a difference between authorized and unauthorized access, nor can there be maintenance of data integrity or availability. That is, the controls required for data integrity are cybersecurity controls. For example, integrity of time reporting data comes from having the staff member whose time is being reported enter and attest to it, the supervisor of that staff member review and attest as well, and the manager accountable for maintaining code of conduct standards checking their figures and attesting to their compliance. All of this is made possible with access control, data security, and incident identification and alerting, all of which are cybersecurity capabilities. The cybersecurity controls are not something else off to the side that can be ratcheted up and down to protect integrity and availability that somehow exist independently of those controls. Inattention to cybersecurity means you literally have none of these other desirable data attributes. This means that every technology manager pays attention to cybersecurity to the extent they feel accountable for data integrity, and as the number of cybersecurity-only managers grows, the technology managers without cybersecurity in their job description become less accountable.

This is symptomatic of the more ubiquitous problem in many organizations called "the silo effect." Where an individual is responsible for only one component of an end-to-end architecture, decisions are hampered by the tendency in large organizations to create departments that specialize, become comfortable in their expertise within a specialty, and evolve their departments around the specialization independently from the goals and mission of the greater organization.[9] Large banks are particularly at risk for the silo effect. In such organizations, cybersecurity is a specialty, and other departments tend to assume that cybersecurity risks are covered because they trust the culture of the greater organization to identify and address them. Product managers worry only about product, network managers worry only about network performance, and these groups often assume that cybersecurity managers are the only ones who should worry about cybersecurity. Nevertheless, CISOs often delegate critical parts of the cybersecurity program to people in these non-security roles. For example, they rely on product managers to identify sensitive data and network managers to understand the purpose of firewall rules. So any lapse on the part of a product manager to identify data elements that are particularly sensitive and/or any oversight on the part of a network manager to understand the purpose of a firewall rule will create vulnerabilities in even the most well-managed cybersecurity programs.

The solution is to hold all managers equally responsible for cybersecurity incidents within their environment. A financial product manager is keenly aware of how criminals may exploit their products for gain and should be including avoidance of detailed threat scenarios in product business requirements. It should then be clear to each technology component owner how controls within their environment contribute to the overall end-to-end features that comprise product defense against those threats. The engineering process and corresponding validation strategies are described in detail in the US National Institute of Standard and Technology standards for Systems Security Engineering.[10]

To understand why such extensive collaboration is required to secure financial systems, consider the common financial transactions supported by an Automated Teller Machine (ATM). These are typically deposit, withdraw, and view balances. Machines themselves are standardized enough to allow for connection to shared industry networks and to allow for industry standard service providers to use the same processes and technology to serve multiple bank clients. Machines are connected to switches that enable secure data transfer and message sequence integrity. In many banks, teller applications were designed prior to the advent of ATM, and they support all operations that would be available via an ATM. So rather than duplicate the programming available in teller applications, the ATM transactions were transformed to the teller application's format, then entered into the legacy teller application via a gateway or screen emulation technology. This means that, even internally, a single ATM transaction may traverse several different technology platforms.

As ATM technology became ubiquitous, there have been more and more security layers added to ATM cards and machines. For example, EMV chips replacing magnetic stripes have been making it harder to commit fraud using the card itself by skimming card information to impersonate a user. In response, ATM attacks have moved to the financial industry's networks. Malware has been introduced directly into ATMs or the ATM network to facilitate fraud schemes.[11] There have also been cases where bank insiders collaborate with each other and/or external fraudsters to steal cash, cards, or data from ATMs. However, cybersecurity programs typically do not include the monitoring of digital controls over cash. Hence, the situation provides a good example of a different way to think about cybersecurity as everyone's responsibility.

Figure 7-6 illustrates the transaction flow between networks and computers at various entities that contribute to ATM services. It is easy to see that multiple organizations build and maintain technology components that enable ATM transactions. While the Bank that owns the ATM may be the same as the Bank Card issuer, it is also common that they are different, as in the example. The end-to-end transaction flow is similar regardless. The transaction begins when a customer authenticates to an ATM machine using information on the card itself. The transaction request must pass through the Bank Owner's Debit Card processor as well as the Card Issuer's Debit Card processor in order to retrieve balances or obtain approval to withdraw cash. There is also a fee settlement process that is not part of the diagram, as it likely would traverse a different network connection.

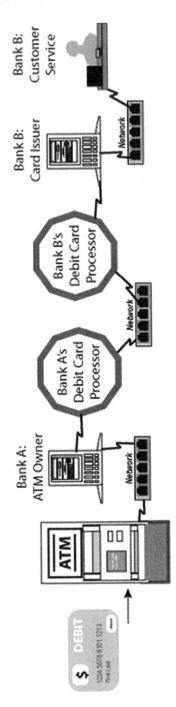

Figure 7-6. ATM illustration

Securing an ATM transaction requires that multiple organizations understand their role in the end-to-end transaction flow and operate accordingly. Each organization specifies business requirements for security at the heart of the bank's operation, and these requirements are implemented in software logic. Integrity failures in checking balances, credit limits, and anomalies in cash dispensing are typically due to software design flaws or bugs not typically covered by cybersecurity programs. However, these situations have repeatedly been the root cause of ATM fraud losses. Even a small bank may have multiple organizations maintaining ATM control points that are important to monitor from a cybersecurity perspective. Organizations in scope of ATM card transaction processing that correspond to the flow of information from the left to the right of Figure 7-6 are listed here, with corresponding systems security responsibilities:

- Card Issuer Product Managers: Distribute cards, address identity theft vulnerabilities in both account opening and re-enrollment.

- ATM Operations: Deliver cash, design and maintain device physical and logical security, maintain and monitor physical security, OR specify and oversee outsourced ATM operation activities.

- Real Estate Facilities Managers: Maintain physical security controls ATM, as well as network connectivity, bank data centers, branch and distributed desktops, network devices and cash in transit.

- Network Operations: Appropriately segregate access to enterprise, extended, and publicly accessible network services to minimize risk of unauthorized access to internal systems (e.g., ensure severed connection from bank may not be taken over by imposter).

- Bank ATM Owner: Manage customer records and interaction with messages requesting approval, ensuring that balances are appropriately updated.

- Bank Database Administrator: Configure confidentiality, integrity, and availability of data and data processing environments.

- Bank Access Administrator: Ensure access to the network, database, and storage infrastructure supporting ATM transactions is restricted to authorized use.

- Bank Security Operations: Ensure alerts and alarms and response procedures for technical security controls in the network, database, and storage infrastructure supporting ATM transactions are implemented and operated in a consistent and comprehensive manner.

- Bank Storage Administrator: Ensure that storage media is encrypted in the ATM, the key and software delivery media to ATM, and on customer data at rest in any platform that supports ATM transactions.

- Bank Technology Risk: Ensure changes in applications, technology infrastructure, systems development life cycle, and operational processes do not result in breaches of technology risk appetite or diminish the effectiveness of existing technology controls.

- Debit Card Processor: Operate messaging, routing, authorization protocols, and fee calculations as per industry participant agreements.

- Bank Card Issuer: Resolve customer complaints and identify root causes of suspicious activities reported by customers, understand liability for fraud, and minimize the percentage of transactions where liability for fraud belongs with the bank.

- ATM Channel Operator: Monitor suppliers to ensure that ATM maintenance is appropriate. Perform frequency and anomaly monitoring to ensure that risk thresholds are not routinely exceeded.

- Bank Human Resources: Ensure that security roles and responsibilities are assigned to every individual via job function. Policy and procedure enforces accountability for compliance with security policy and consequences for non-compliance include dismissal.

- Bank Lawyers: Ensure that asset protection requirements are included in contracts with third parties handling assets held offsite and enforced for those who are onsite. Identify regulations that apply to the business and require the incorporation of security controls in order to meet requirements and ensure that they identified and included in Security Program requirements.

- Bank Accountants: Maintain controls over financial reporting with respect to ATM services.

Note the last few roles are important to the bank's internal control environment required to support ATM services, though in time sequence, they fall off the right-hand side of the diagram in Figure 7-6. Consider application of this example of end-to-end transaction architecture for all possible transactions supported by the financial institution, and it is easy to see why literally every manager in a firm plays a role in maintaining cybersecurity. Also note the CIO and development staff obviously have development and deployment responsibilities that would be prerequisite, or to the left, of the sequential diagram.

Many bank employees are familiar with posters proclaiming, "*Cybersecurity is everyone's responsibility.*" These typically feature a distraught employee tackling a computer virus and include an enterprise-wide employee level control instruction like "*Don't click on suspicious links!*" or "*Choose hard passwords!*" But hard passwords are not an enterprise-wide capability. They are an example of a control delegated to multiple access control administrators. Where cybersecurity is taken seriously as an enterprise-wide capability, every manager would be making their own list of what they can do to develop and maintain cybersecurity controls within their own area of responsibility. That is, the ATM Channel owner would not leave software security to the assessment teams but would employ managers who utilize secure software design and coding standards on their development teams and constantly be on the lookout for new securing algorithm designs that make the best use of modern key authentication technology. By contrast, in practice, many banks missed the MasterCard deadline to convert ATMs from magnetic strips to EMV technology through inattention to basic business requirements, and consequently lost more money to fraud than the cost of the required technology upgrades.

Monitoring and Reporting

In the shorter term, while the financial industry awaits needed cultural improvement to have enterprise-wide cybersecurity capabilities in place, it relies on checklist-enabled assessments such as the Federal Financial Institutions Examination Council (FFIEC) Cybersecurity Assessment Tool (CAT), and corresponding vulnerability testing. Unfortunately, these "gap analysis" approaches promote a mindset that existing controls are adequately designed and simply need to be enumerated. The execution of such assessments is often delegated to junior staff with little familiarity of either business or technology operations. The methodology is often manual, based on interviews with stakeholders. Where such assessments are performed without reference to actual financial transactions, they perpetuate maintenance of a set of controls that appear to be adequately designed while skipping a step critical to any cybersecurity assessment: that of validating the effectiveness of controls as designed.[12]

Even if control effectiveness could be taken for granted, these enterprise-wide assessment capabilities would only be actually effective if all processes at risk from cybersecurity threats are included to the extent required to understand how systems support them. All such systems that support each process would need to be defined at the level required to understand what cybersecurity controls protect, detect, and respond to regarding threats to the businesses that use those systems. Hence, if there is one place to start to verify the effectiveness of a cybersecurity program, it is to develop an accurate view of current state.

In organizations that have not invested in process definition, this view will be challenging and will require investment in some shared representation of business process to which all stakeholders agree. In organizations that have invested in process definition, this view can be assembled by connecting process flows to the underlying technology. Of course, in both cases, the processes may not be detailed enough to recognize all the technology control points. In this case, even organizations that have embraced formal business process definitions will have some work to do to bring them to the level of detail required to link them to technology that is used to execute them. Often this will start with a simple classification of the technology into business processes based on the organization for which a technology component was ordered. Lists are circulated to business technology liaisons (who commence investigations to see who is actually using the device or software), corrections are made, and an iterative investigation becomes the starting point for a link between business process and actual technology.

It is important in this stage of assignment of technology to business function to preserve the same nomenclature that the technologists use to represent devices and software, or to evolve it to an industry standard such as the NIST Official Common Platform Enumeration (CPE) Dictionary.[13] That is, a financial institution must have standards on how to represent technology with data; this way of describing technology with data is *technology meta-data*.

Process definition using technology meta-data requires a framework approach to technical component enumeration, structured formalization, and communication across the enterprise. It requires combined contribution of managers who are process owners, technology owners, and risk management professionals. It facilitates an architectural approach to risk identification and may require skills development and continuous growth for staff at all levels of experience, in technical and non-technical roles. This includes education and development on institution-specific technology topics, such as entrenched networks and application systems, but also instruction on the nature and functionality of emerging threats.

Whether communicated across the enterprise, technology managers use systems to link technology to business. This is done primarily for financial reasons, to justify budget for space, machines, and people. Building locations, hardware serial numbers, software licenses, and technology headcount are routinely associated with accounting cost codes, and these correspond to business budgets. Business leaders who are technology-savvy have learned to question the values of each item included in a cost-coded budget and develop methods for understanding the contribution of the item to the business technology capability. While such billing data can be relied upon to identify each device or piece of software they are required to support, a business leader may also factor in business internal headcount they dedicate to interface with technology organizations.

However, in practice such financial accounting meta-data is often not reliable. For example, cost codes used to record equipment purchases remain with the equipment despite an upgrade wherein the business application was transferred to a shared environment. That shared environment may have been purchased by a different business that now assumes the cost burden (unintentionally) of the applications of another business's process. Similarly, software licensed to the original purchaser may still be associated with that business in inventory, despite the fact that actual billing has been changed to utilize a per-user cost model based on entitlements to use the software. Without a purposeful meta-data design, tracing from technology to business process usage can become a challenging forensic exercise.

While every business executive has a charter and a responsibility to deliver value to the firm, and every cybersecurity executive is highly confident that their own skills and experience can carry the burden of delivery for tools and techniques required to keep the threats at bay, the ground truth is that people work for the person who pays them. Every day, every person at work has to decide the task they will perform. If days are filled with demands to deliver software and this can be accomplished without following all the governance practices required to create and maintain the meta-data describing how technology enables financial transactions, then that is what will happen.

It is very difficult to design an organization that can't break rules without management's awareness. Note that a situation in which everyone knows rules are broken is not the same as detection and acknowledgment that the rules have been broken. Business documentaries abound wherein both corporate directives and laws were broken and detected en masse in situations where no single staff member felt responsible to call attention to the violations. For example, telecommunications engineers at Enron knew that there was no product for sale that would boost bandwidth as advertised in investor memorandums, and accountants on the audit team at Arthur Anderson knew that there were material misstatements in Enron's financial reporting[14]. For a financial industry example, Equifax's failure to patch a known, severe internet cybersecurity vulnerability was, according to the former Equifax CEO, a process execution failure by cyber operations staff[15]. However, a broader question remains: wasn't there any executive similarly accountable for the integrity of the firm's information systems who was empowered to ensure capability effectiveness in patching and to raise the issue of process weaknesses?[16]

Note the word "empowered" is key here. Where employees are sorted into functional silos, they may opine only on firm operations for which they are directly responsible. Inexperience on the part of a cybersecurity officer that results in control gaps may therefore go unnoticed by peer organizations, who may see the output of the security program but not how it is architected. On the other hand, the silo effect does not prevent the inadequacies of a program from being actively ridiculed at the lower levels, with the consequence that cybersecurity policies are routinely ignored. This observation is not in any way meant to give credence to those managers who actively seek to thwart the goals of the cybersecurity program simply because they can. But it is offered in acknowledgement that the cybersecurity officer (by whatever title the office is known; e.g., CISO) is expected to be both a jack-of-all-trades in the organization and a master at technology risk and control.

Like the CIO, a CISO is expected to see across all technologies and appreciate the strength and weaknesses of the controls capabilities in each to contribute to an overall end-to-end maintenance of confidentiality, integrity, and availability of information throughout the firm. In a small firm, this person is usually chosen for their technical acumen. In a large firm, it is sometimes acknowledged that negotiations on technical configurations across large groups of highly talented and opinionated engineers is a negotiation challenge, in which case, the decision criteria by which the incumbent is judged may focus on social skills. This situation may be appropriate if there is sufficient security expertise and independence among delegates to committees charged with maintaining control effectiveness.

Where there is clear connection between business process and technology components, not only cost, but all aspects of control accountability are unavoidable. Businesses that understand how technology supports their processes with control points can request reports and alerts that allow them to monitor the performance of technology controls. Clear-cut accountability for technology operation promotes awareness of cybersecurity responsibility among senior technology managers and prompts them to designate roles and responsibilities for managing cybersecurity risk within their domain of responsibility. Where there is shared understanding that controls are weak due to poor design or performance, business people and technology professionals can have meaningful conversations about upgrades to reduce risk to an acceptable residual level. It is the metadata architecture that allows this to happen. Transparent communication enabling shared understanding of current state of security is the best remedy for the silo effect.

Unlike a Zachman-like framework that seeks to fully describe the same thing from different angles, a meta-data approach fully describes end-to-end processing. It is a system view of the financial service, following the International Council on Systems Engineering (INCOSE) definition of a system as a *"construct or collection of different elements that together produce results not obtainable by the elements alone."*[17] The system view is described using meta-data from all contributing components, including people, processes, and technology that compose the system as a whole. To produce a system view requires a coordinated approach to describing operations that combines all operational data sources–for example, digital identity Repository, role-based access control (RBAC), business process models (BPMs), a technology configuration management database

(CMDB), and an automated incident management application. Figure 7-7 identifies the primary data element that is created within an exemplar set of operation support applications and the direction of data propagation throughout the other applications. Although each application may be expected to have its own requirements process and systems development life cycle, it is necessary to have close coordination in maintaining the integrity of the data elements in order to have an appropriate response to security incident. If resources are not expended to ensure that events detected by the incident management system can be immediately and accurately associated with people, technology, and business process, they will no doubt be expended in the form of forensic expenses in the incident response process.

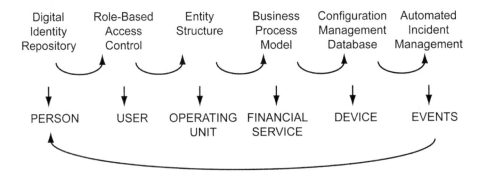

Figure 7-7. *Architecture meta-data*

Although resource allocation for the cybersecurity program is typically delegated to the CISO, each significant management entity in a financial services organization plays a role in maintaining the integrity of meta-data used to secure systems and to detect and respond to incidents. The level of involvement required to be effective is commensurate with the contribution to the integrity of the information in these critical repositories. Figure 7-8 lists the roles involved in ATM deployment as enumerated earlier and identifies the application that creates meta-data where the role may be expected to have responsibility for data integrity and accuracy. It also provides three types of metrics that we would expect to be consumed by individuals in the respective role, regardless of whether their efforts helped produced them. It is obvious from Figure 7-8 that there is organizational cross-reliance on data integrity in areas well beyond cybersecurity. Where these systems shared attributes, it is possible to associate event logs and business activity data with a wide variety of corporate information that will provide metrics on financial services operations, performance, projects, deployments, maintenance, training, testing, and retirement. In this context, all stakeholders easily understand cybersecurity metrics, and cybersecurity risk monitoring can therefore become a shared responsibility. That is, it should be clear that each of these organizations must allocate resources to ensure that the data they create that makes its way into the Automated Incident Management application is serviceable for the purpose of cybersecurity.

Role:	ATM Channel Operator	ATM Operations	Bank Security Operations
Meta-Data Integrity Responsibility:	Role-Based Access Control	Configuration Management Database	Incident Management Automation
Meta-Data Oversight Responsibility:	Incident Management Automation	Incident Management Automation	Digital Identity Repository
ATM Metrics Consumption:	projects, operations, maintenance	deployments, maintenance, retirement	operations, testing, maintenance

Figure 7-8. *Sources and uses for metrics based on shared meta-data*

Metrics

In the evaluation of Enterprise Architecture, cybersecurity can be measured at a component level, a holistic level, and an end-to-end transaction level. Although the meta-data structure of metrics data will differ with custom business process models and operating unit structures, technology controls themselves are defined in terms of functional control capabilities and can be tested independently of the business they are used to control. A failure identified in the control testing would then reflect back on the business process that utilized the control, just as the performance metrics of a business application reflect its utility to the business.

Key to the insight that cybersecurity is a property of EA is recognition that cybersecurity *can be measured* as a property of EA *whether it has been planned as such*. That is, it is very easy for external control professionals to trace a financial transaction through the operational processes and systems that produce it and provide *assessments* of whether management control may be bypassed at any point in the process. They start with the business process and interview people who use the technology, then find the technologists who support the technology, and reconcile data used by the business with the applications that produce it. If there is a plan for how the transaction is secured within the process, and documentation exists, a control professional will use the documents. If not, they will document the system security, as they understand it, given their research. In some cases, the work papers of an external auditor contain better system descriptions than the documentation used by the company itself. Either way, it is hoped that the system description includes cybersecurity controls that, if properly implemented, should suffice to secure the transaction. If not, a professional assesor will report a control gap. Whether or not there are gaps, all controls will be verified to see if they work as described.

The most reliable assessment tool available to the financial, or any other industry, for cybersecurity testing is an independent audit. There are two types of audits: compliance and substantive.[18] Compliance audits begin with a documented process for achieving a security goal and tests that the process has been implemented with no relevant exceptions. Substantive audits begin with a content description of secure system configuration and tests to ensure that the configuration is correctly implemented. Compliance audits can be based on checklists and interviews, but substantive audits always measure a given TTOA on its conformance to technical specifications. Both are *verification* tests, as they compare the variables in the configuration files to a set of values for those variables that have been previously determined to thwart perpetrators. Verification tests are often supplemented with a *validation* test, meant to provide a basis for assessing the future behavior of a system based on its current behavior.

An example of verification that measures compliance with technical specifications is the Payment Card Industry Data Security Standard (PCI-DSS).[19] The scope of the standard is data that is used to process credit card payments. The criteria for security attribution range from building a secure network to maintaining an information security policy. The tests range from sampling system components as TTOAs to observing systems operators executing incident response procedures. The test result is a worksheet completed by the assessor indicating the extent of system compliance with the PCIS-DSS standard.

An example of validation that is expected to predict secure behavior is a penetration test; a hacker for hire uses criminal and espionage techniques to attempt to bypass system security controls. If the system behavior thwarts the attack, it passes the behavioral test. Note that this does not necessarily mean it will survive a real attack. Think of it as getting a driver's license. If someone passes the test, they are qualified to drive a car but still may end up in an accident due to situations not encountered in the test environment.

The term *Target of Assessment*, or *Technical Target of Assessment*
(TTOA), is a generic label for the system as configured and tested, no
matter how many technical components it may contain.[20] As illustrated
in the generic cybersecurity control descriptions in Figure 7-9, a TTOA
definition can also be independent of the system it is designed to support.
The basic metrics for and tests of management control over technology are
the same for similar operating systems, database management systems,
and off-the-shelf software; however, today's custom business application
environments are so diverse that every firm has to design their own *system-
level* security model and associated TTOA set of features, configurations,
and internal testing criteria. Note that although both internal and external
auditors use a financial institution's own documentation to understand the
system security model, they independently devise their own tests to verify
and validate that the assessment target meets control objectives required
by the business process.

CONTROL STRATEGY	*Data*	*Operating System*	*Application*	*Network*	*Workstation*
PREVENTION	DBMS login, Key-based application authentication, Field encryption	Centralized Identity and Access Management (IAM), Segregation of admin duties	IAM, Fine-grained Entitlements, Encrypted sessions	Handheld authentication, Session-based filters, Private encrypted links	IAM, Antivirus, Intrusion prevention
DETECTION	Logs in centralized repository	File integrity checking, Rogue process detection	Anomaly monitoring, Fraud detection	Link and utilization monitoring, Data loss detection	Intrusion detection
RECOVERY	Storage mirroring	Cluster technology	Hot standby	Redundant alternative routing	Automated imaging

Figure 7-9. *Generic TTOA cybersecurity controls*

One of the issues complicating the application of measurement to the property of security is a question of scope. Technical tests and metrics for TTOAs are concerned with components rather than the system as a whole. To make claims for security at the system level, risk managers typically aggregate TTOA component measures. But where the TTOAs measured are components of a larger system, it is often a subject of debate on how the security content of the targets contribute to a conclusion that the system as a whole is secure. This debate has a long history and shows no signs of being resolved soon.[21] There is no current agreed-upon substitute for devising a custom rationale for how the business process may be claimed to be secure based on the assessments at the component level.

Another complication for TTOA metrics is that systems generally include operators who have the ability to accomplish configuration changes. It is hard to assess content validity with respect to our definition of security in an environment where changes are frequent for threat as well as the configuration. For example, the configuration variables may be set so only authorized software is running on the machine. However, if authorized software has security bugs or flaws due to either a mistake in a software update or an emerging threat, then the content validation may pass but will not accurately measure security. Also, there may be situations where one organization is exposed to threats that are not faced by another organization. In these cases, TTOA configuration metrics may only be internally valid–that is, they might be completely applicable in the sample of software under examination but not extensible to the system-level end-to-end transaction process to which conclusions might reasonably be extended in a different environment.

However, there are industry standards for governance and oversight of any financial operational process, and these apply to technology control processes. The Bank of International Settlements (BIS) Basel Committee guidance for Operational Risk–Supervisory Guidelines for the Advanced

Measurement Approaches is extremely relevant to this topic.[22] Although cybersecurity teams typically place high confidence in their internal tools, techniques, and incident response procedures, there remains a real risk the cybersecurity program itself may be inadequate. Therefore it is no surprise Basel guidance would stipulate there be clear and measurable objectives for its verification and validation activities. These include critical analysis of the very framework upon which the verification and validation measurement itself is devised. For example, the framework design should ensure the availability, expertise, and independence of the reviewers. These are highly customized to each financial institution's organizational characteristics, its board influence, and the experience of senior management. There is no off-the-shelf product or certification for any one framework or method of testing any set of internal controls, and cybersecurity is no exception.

Nevertheless, there appears to be broad agreement from regulators that verification and validation work on cybersecurity should be documented and the results distributed to stakeholders in management, internal audit, and risk committees. Reporting should include known issues, scenario analysis results, cybersecurity incidents that occurred in similarly organized competitors, and updates on project management of any corrective action plans intended to resolve gaps and weaknesses. Details should be summarized and periodically reported to the board of directors, or an appropriate risk or audit committee. These reports should include enumeration of potential consequences from any weaknesses or deviation from policy, procedures, laws, and/or regulations. This information should prompt discussion and debate on the best management approach to address. The Chief Risk Officer or equivalent is ultimately responsible for understanding the business impact of cybersecurity metrics and will often be asked to attest to the effectiveness of a financial institution's overall risk management framework, into which the cybersecurity framework should be incorporated. Ideally, all those with decision-making responsibility that impacts the firm's cybersecurity posture will contribute to that framework. Ideally, the cybersecurity team would have done the research into the firm's Operational Risk Management Framework to be able to promote and assist in that integration as requisite.

Moving Ahead

This chapter considered the impact of cybersecurity risk management decisions across the enterprise architecture. The architectural perspective can prove extremely useful to illustrate the interaction of various risk management decisions that have driven expanded investment in the name of improved cybersecurity controls. Once architecture has been enhanced to counter observed risks, however, management ideally should increase attention on indicators that modifications to architectural components (such as changes to personnel and technology) have resulted in improved organizational preparedness against cybersecurity threats.

The next chapter explores the concept of enterprise capabilities. Enterprises continuously make investments in new technologies and personnel. However, as the next chapter illustrates, management should consider if their investment has made the company more capable in executing the cyber mission. The upcoming chapter analyzes the nature of organizational cybersecurity capabilities and explores ways the enterprise can build cybersecurity capability effectiveness to achieve maximum value from the investment in architecture.

Notes

1. ThreatTrack (2015). "CISO Role Still in Flux: Despite
    Small Gains, CISOs Face an Uphill Battle in the
    C-Suite." retrieved in October 2017 from `https://`
    `www.threattrack.com/getmedia/5d310c4c-aed6-`
    `4633-929f-0b5903d2bc79/CISO-Role-Still-in-`
    `Flux.aspx`

2. Federal Deposit Insurance Corporation, Information
    Technology Strategic Plan: 2017-202, pg. 6. See:
    `https://www.fdic.gov/about/strategic/it_`
    `plan/fdic_information_technology_strategic_`
    `plan_2017-2020.pdf` and `https://www.fdic.gov/`
    `about/strategic/it_plan/appendixaglossary.`
    `html`. Note, the FDIC adopted this definition
    from Gartner, see: `http://www.gartner.com/it-`
    `glossary/enterprise-architecture-ea/`,

3. Federal Financial Institutions Examination Council
    (2015). FFIEC IT Examination Handbook - IT
    Management Booklet, p. 9.

4. Ibid.

5. Zachman, John, "A Framework for Information
    Systems Architecture," *IBM Systems Journal*, Vol. 26
    No. 3, 1987.

6. The Open Group. 2018. TOGAF Architecture
    Development Method. `http://www.opengroup.`
    `org/subjectareas/enterprise/togaf`

7. Sherwood, John, Andrew Clark, and David Lynas,
    Enterprise Security Architecture, (San Francisco, CA:
    CMP Books, 2005).

8. Bayuk, Jennifer, *Enterprise Security for the Executive, Setting the Tone from the Top*, (Westport, CT: Praeger, 2010), p. 122.

9. Tett, Gillian, *The Silo Effect, The Peril of Expertise and the Promise of Breaking Down Barriers*, (New York: Simon & Schuster, 2015).

10. Ross, R., McEvilley, M. and Oren, J., Systems Security Engineering, Considerations for a Multidisciplinary Approach in the Engineering of Trustworthy Secure Systems, US National Institute of Standard and Technology, 2016, available at: https://doi.org/10.6028/NIST.SP.800-160.

11. ATM Marketplace, "ATM Future Trends Report," Network Media Group, 2017, pg54, see https://www.atmmarketplace.com

12. Rohmeyer, Ben-Zvi, Lombardi, Maltz (2017). Capability Effectiveness Testing for Architectural Resiliency in Financial Systems. PICMET 2017. Conference Session – Resilience of Systems. Stevens Institute of Technology.

13. https://nvd.nist.gov/products/cpe

14. McLean, Bethany and Peter Elkind, *The Smartest Guys in the Room: The Amazing Rise and Scandalous Fall of Enron*, (New York, NY: Portfolio Trade, 2003).

15. Shepardson, Dave, Oct. 2, 2017, "Equifax failed to patch security vulnerability in March: former CEO, https://www.reuters.com/article/us-equifax-breach/equifax-failed-to-patch-security-vulnerability-in-march-former-ceo-idUSKCN1C71VY

16. Office of Senator Elizabeth Warren "Bad Credit: Uncovering Equifax's Failure to Protect Americans' Personal Information," February 2018. https://www.documentcloud.org/documents/4368610-Equifax-Report-Interactive-FINAL.html

17. Definition of the International Council on Systems Engineering (INCOSE), posted at http://www.incose.org/AboutSE/WhatIsSE, retrieved December 1, 2017.

18. Bayuk, J., *Stepping Through the IS Audit, A Guide for Information Systems Managers, Second Edition.* 2005: Information Systems Audit and Control Association.

19. Payment Card Industry (PCI) Security Standards Council, *Payment Card Industry (PCI) Data Security Standard*, Version 3.2. 2016,

20. Common Criteria Recognition Agreement, Common Criteria for Information Technology Security Evaluation Version 3.1. 2009.

21. Schneider, F.B., ed. *Trust in Cyberspace.* 1999, National Research Council, National Academy Press.

    Neumann, P.G., *Principled Assuredly Trustworthy Composable Architectures.* 2004, SRI International.

22. Basel Committee on Banking Supervision, Operational Risk –Supervisory Guidelines for the Advanced Measurement Approaches, 2011, www.bis.org

CHAPTER 8

How Can We Improve Our Capabilities?

Discussion about cybersecurity often focuses on observed risk dimensions or associated control strategies devised in response to observed risks. However, optimizing enterprise cybersecurity risk reduction is a more general capability essential to minimizing cybersecurity risk. McKinsey and Company have described organizational capability as "anything an organization does well that drives meaningful business results." Ideally, recognized strategic priorities, such as cybersecurity risk reduction, should be supported with organizational capabilities and appropriate actions taken to create and continuously develop capabilities aligned with such strategic priorities. A valuable contribution of independent observers such as McKinsey has been to notice that this alignment is sometimes lacking.[1] As described in Chapter 7, such alignment can be achieved with an architectural view that describes a comprehensive, largely top-down approach intended to drive the organization toward enterprise cybersecurity decisions that are consistent with organizational goals. An architecture view strengthens communication on strategy and informs the selection of the "right" things to do, with respect to identification and execution of projects to build desired capabilities. Although successful project execution provides verification that plans for security measures have

© Paul Rohmeyer, Jennifer L. Bayuk 2019
P. Rohmeyer and J. L. Bayuk, *Financial Cybersecurity Risk Management*,
https://doi.org/10.1007/978-1-4842-4194-3_8

been accomplished, there is recognition of the need for more substantive validation that security architecture achieves security goals. The National Institute of Standards and Technology (NIST) characterizes this distinction as correctness versus effectiveness.[2] From an architecture perspective, verification is the determination that a system is "built right," while validation determines that the "right system was built."[3] The validation question is meant to assist in the determination that the resulting architecture does what we intended it to do. In other words, it is how we know that our capabilities actually accomplished our goals for reducing risk. It is how we can be sure they drive meaningful results in the organization. It is how we continuously monitor and develop our capabilities for continuous improvement and respond to emerging threats. In short, we need to "get real," so to speak, in our planning as well as in our execution. Cybersecurity is not a domain that tolerates theoretical attribution based on a project plan; enterprise capabilities are only relevant when applied to real-world conditions.

Build a Learning Organization

Enterprise knowledge development can be driven only by individual commitment to continuous learning. Most of us have probably observed experienced, successful professionals express frustration with the need to keep pace with continuous technology change. Cybersecurity, however, is a domain that can be complex, change rapidly, and trigger events of high impact. It therefore requires thoughtful evaluation of, and commitment to, ongoing, lifelong learning.

The domain of knowledge management (KM) provides important guidance in building organizations that foster a culture of continuous learning to drive enterprise change and innovation. Organizations that rely on the intellectual capabilities of "knowledge workers" should expect to invest in building architectures to support them. This includes adopting an effective organizational design, marshaling supportive leadership, and fostering behaviors that promote continuous learning.[4]

In their classic book *The Knowledge-Creating Company*, authors Nonaka and Takeuchi presented a theory of organizational learning that has broadly influenced the KM domain.[5] They described how the interplay between theoretical constructs (such as models) and real-world experiences drives a cycle of enterprise knowledge creation. They showed how individual knowledge is spread through the enterprise via a socialization process that provides vital feedback to many individuals who, in turn, drive subsequent knowledge conversion cycles via socialization through a larger audience.

This process of knowledge creation is presented as vital to driving competitive advantage by moving individualized, internal knowledge into external representations that can be shared across the organization, enabling further improvement through exposure to a group. Individuals included in the socialization re-internalize the new knowledge, perhaps resulting in the creation of new potential innovations. The organizational learning cycle, applied to the domain of cybersecurity, provides a method for the intellectual capabilities of one team member (individual knowledge) to be shared across the enterprise. Nonaka and Takeuchi specified five phases of "Knowledge Creation" as:

1. Sharing Tacit Knowledge

2. Creating Concepts

3. Justifying Concepts

4. Building an Archetype

5. Cross-Leveling of Knowledge

In each phase, Knowledge Creation is accomplished via four essential modes:

A. Socialization

B. Externalization

C. Combination

D. Internalization

By applying this theory to real-world conditions on the cybersecurity landscape, we can identify potential opportunities to build a cybersecurity culture that promotes continuous learning. The following considerations may help illustrate current limitations as well as the possibilities for building a learning culture.

- *Break Down Organizational Silos*: Cybersecurity is a multidisciplinary topic, and therefore we need to provide opportunities for cross-functional teams to move through the four knowledge creation modes.

- *Ensure Knowledge is Shared:* The organizational investment in threat intelligence and other data feeds may be maximized by ensuring knowledge creation phases and modes are enabled. Similarly, the actual data produced by technical scans, log files, and other sensors will only contribute to enterprise learning if shared, studied, and socialized. Such a process simply will not happen without management's support and guidance.

- *Mix Theoretical and Hands-On Learning:* The model presented by Nonaka and Takeuchi illustrates the vital need to provide learning that combines classroom/ textbook delivery with opportunities for real-world application. Consider that perhaps a better way to train beginner penetration testers is to send them to ethical hacker training and, upon completion, immediately conduct an actual test within your organization of which your senior staff will observe, discuss, and maybe learn something themselves.

- *Work Beyond Organizational Boundaries:* There may also be opportunities to apply organizational learning concepts beyond the constraints of a single enterprise. Consider how current cyber information sharing enterprises are currently structured and the perceived lack of effectiveness. Understanding the requirements for knowledge creation may provide important clues to increasing the value of participation in Information Sharing and Analysis Centers (ISACs)[6] and to developing shared understandings of risk across business partnerships.

Improve the Quality of Risk Assessments

Cybersecurity risks are routinely identified in the course of strategic planning, compliance activities, and operational experience. Software-aided cybersecurity assessment tools have made it relatively easy for organizations to compare their cybersecurity programs to standards, regulations, and best practices. Automated configuration management systems and patch management tools have made it relatively easy for administrators to know when they have publicly known vulnerabilities. For those who do not have in-house assessment processes, a proliferation of independent cybersecurity assessment service providers have made strategic use of such software to create situational awareness for their clients. For decades there have been such tools in internal audit and operational risk departments, referred to as Governance Risk and Control (GRC) tools, and many have been extended to incorporate cybersecurity assessments using application and infrastructure cybersecurity metrics.

Such systematic capture of cybersecurity issues is extremely important, but the issue list has very limited utility in the absence of a description of the business process that may be impacted. Whether or not the issues indicate risk that is intolerable, or even that one system presents more risk than another, can only be decided in the context of risk appetite, tolerance, and threshold measures. It is important for financial institutions to start with business process as an anchor when identifying inherent risk, and to base inherent risk impact parameters on the value of the process to the business and its customers, rather than on some generic cybersecurity standard.

A business process that is material to the institution's bottom line is typically assumed to have a higher inherent risk than one that does not. Because many financial institutions have a large number of business systems, it is common practice to focus detailed risk estimations on only "high-risk" systems, where high risk is assumed to be based on criticality of the underlying business process. Unfortunately, the criteria for labeling applications *"high risk"* is often not articulated beyond a vague reference to proximity to business process. Such methodology, in effect, assumes prior to the risk analysis that systems that are tightly integrated with business process will be the ones that need improvements to produce an acceptable level of overall cybersecurity residual risk.

For example, in some financial institutions, every application is required to undergo multiple types of assessments, and "risk" ratings vary by assessment domain. Though assessment names and rating scales vary widely across organizations, Figure 8-1 shows a typical example of Information Classification, Information Vulnerability, and Resiliency Assessment rating scales. The outcome of each assessment type is typically an ordinal measure on a scale specific to the assessment.

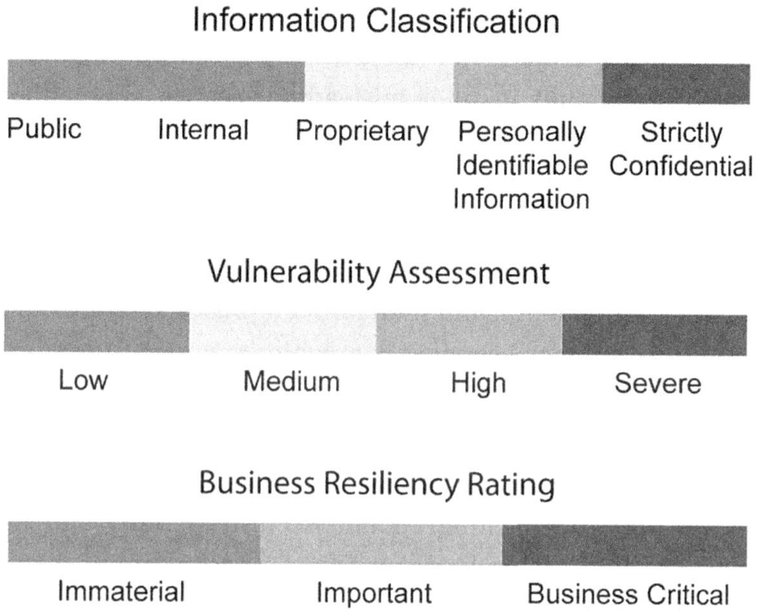

Information Classification

| Public | Internal | Proprietary | Personally Identifiable Information | Strictly Confidential |

Vulnerability Assessment

| Low | Medium | High | Severe |

Business Resiliency Rating

| Immaterial | Important | Business Critical |

Figure 8-1. *Ordinal value assessment outcomes*

In the example, the Information Classification scale has five values (Public, Internal, Proprietary, Personally Identifiable Information, Strictly Confidential); the Information Vulnerability review scale has four values (Low, Medium, High, Severe); and the Resiliency Assessment scale has three values (Immaterial, Important, Business Critical). Although institutions will have their own labels and internal criteria for assigning these values, and some will have additional assessments, it is typically figures like these that underlie inherent risk ratings assigned to technology. The unit of measure is typically a business application, and there is significant due diligence to ensure that all technology can be associated with a business application and that each business application undergoes each assessment.

Figure 8-2 shows how an application's assessment outcomes are typically combined to come up with an inherent risk rating for an application. The way an application typically gets a risk rating is to assign weights to various assessment results and assign the label "*high risk*" to those whose combined assessments results in the highest values. Such approaches are often misleading because applications that are most critical to the business are not necessarily those with the highest cybersecurity risk. For example, if "*business critical*" translates to monetary value, then it is possible that an analyst considering a system that is comprised of few assets and has relatively minor market value will find it immaterial and therefore not "*business critical*." That would lead some financial services companies to not consider the office building real estate systems they provide to corporate departments as a "*critical*" business systems because they are not a financial services product, cost little, and have less market value. This has the consequence that some heating, cooling, security, lighting, and alarm systems are overlooked in cybersecurity impact assessments that focus on business criticality.

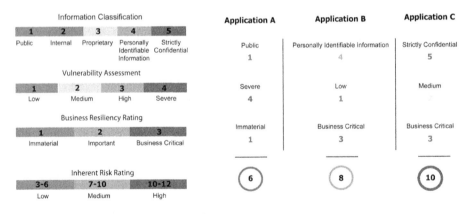

Figure 8-2. *Risk rating calculations*

This oversight is particularly blinding when the systems support a data center. Notice the similarity of that case to the values assigned to Application A in Figure 8-2. This application has severe vulnerabilities, and yet the system is rated low risk. In many institutions, due to time and resource constraints, a vulnerability assessment would not be performed at all on systems considered low risk, so these vulnerabilities would not even show up in the inherent risk rating. Also, there is an argument that any system with "*severe*" vulnerabilities should be considered an organizational weak link, and therefore high risk as a potential launch point to the internal network. Figure 8-2 indicates that where a system has only publicly available information and is immaterial from a business perspective, the high risk label would not be given. Hence it has been difficult for cybersecurity risk professionals in this organization to specify exactly which systems should be graced with the label "*high risk.*" Also observe from Figure 8-2 that an application with "Personally Identifiable Information" and is "Immaterial" from a resiliency perspective would not receive a label of "*high risk.*"

At this stage in our digital evolution, most financial institutions rely on these abstract approaches to risk ratings. Critics of the approach dismiss it as "math using ordinal values," a management consulting approach well-known to yield dubious results.[7] From the perspective of decision-making related to risk, this is the first challenge: to understand on what basis risks have been identified and to make the best use of available information in assigning priorities to risk treatments. Where an institution has a mature scenario-driven approach to cybersecurity risk evaluation, business risk analysis should take precedence over mathematical algorithms applied to the results of label-driven assessments.

Rather than chance that some pure taxonomical classification provides the basis for discounting potentially negative effects of a cybersecurity breach, it is best to run all business systems through cybersecurity risk event scenario analysis at least at some high level of abstraction before coming to the conclusion that some systems are less critical than others in the event of a cyber attack. At the systems level, where systems include people and process as well as technology, all business processes should undergo thorough scenario analysis as described in Chapter 3 and 4. Only by confronting the threat in combination with vulnerability can risk in excess of appetite be identified at a level of detail that allows risk treatments to be formulated to reduce risk to an acceptable residual level (as described in Chapter 6). Cybersecurity risks identified as unique to individual business processes all should be minimized to an acceptable residual level by the cybersecurity program holistically, as the appearance of one issue that highlights a previously unknown vulnerability may raise the priority of a business process with lower inherent risk to the top of the priority list for cybersecurity program improvements.

Even the cybersecurity industry standard most focused on pure cybersecurity operations, the NIST Cybersecurity Framework, begins its discussion of cybersecurity risk identification with the acknowledgement of the *uniqueness* of business process:

To manage cybersecurity risks, a clear understanding of the organization's business drivers and security considerations specific to its use of technology is required. Because each organization's risks, priorities, and systems are unique, along with its use of technology, the tools and methods used to achieve the outcomes described by the Framework will vary. Self-assessment and measurement should improve decision making about investment priorities.[8]

Efforts to improve the quality and depth of risk management standards continue, and organizations would do well to continuously monitor the changing landscape. For example, the Factor Analysis of Information Risk (FAIR) Institute stated a mission to *"Establish and promote information risk management best practices that empower risk professionals to collaborate with their business partners on achieving the right balance between protecting the organization and running the business."*[9] Business alignment goals require common business context, consistent risk language, and a common understanding of foundational risk concepts, which may be developed via the knowledge creating mechanisms described earlier. Furthermore, better guidance on risk quantification techniques, a specific goal of FAIR, would serve to improve business-cybersecurity dialog, understanding, and therefore internal socialization.

Use Organizational Knowledge

Notice that the breakdown of inherent risk labels in Figure 8-2 is not an even split across the continuum of possible values from the lowest possible score, 3, to the highest, 12. There is no even three-way split in these values, and the bulk of the values (the four intervals from three to six) are classified as low risk. These types of sliding scales should always be questioned. It is very common for cybersecurity managers to set the breakpoints between risk ratings with a keen eye toward the requirements that security policies and standards have been specified for applications with certain risk ratings. That is, it is very common for a security standard to require that all medium- and high-risk applications must undergo a software vulnerability scan prior to every production release.

A CISO with a resource-constrained vulnerability scanning team may be tempted to move the scale even further to the left in the face of those requirements. This situation may even present itself in cases where the cybersecurity program has 100 percent management support and virtually unlimited budgets. There are not enough trained cybersecurity professionals in the world, nor enough efficiency and effectiveness in state-of-the-art vulnerability scanning tools, to cover the needs of the financial industry to thoroughly scan every critical application. CISOs are constantly exercising judgment to allocate controls based on their capacity to provide them as opposed to the business' need.

The temptation to measure risk based on the ability to perform against current policies and standards is unfortunately much stronger than any temptation to change policies and standards to emphasize controls over end-to-end security of business transactions. There will always be new security vulnerabilities, and CISOs that are focused on short-term ("bolt-on") situational improvements rather than longer-term architectural ones. Note that this phenomenon is not confined to cybersecurity or even the financial industry. Studies have shown that people often make short-term decisions without understating that they themselves are accountable for consequences.[10] In the technology industry, this situation is exacerbated by the fact that it is very common to change jobs every few years.

In large global financial institutions, managers are actually **_encouraged_** to "rotate," which means a major activity in their day-to-day job performance is devoted to acquiring and demonstrating talents required by their next assignment rather than their current one. This rotating responsibility has the effect that individuals are responsible for very short-term horizons and are not actively encouraged or financially motivated to influence firm stability for longer than the next performance evaluation and bonus cycle, knowing that they personally will not bear the consequences of, nor even be asked to defend, decisions made only a few years earlier.

Motivating improvements in cybersecurity requires cultivation of a culture wherein success is measured in long-term improvements. Short-term visuals like turning vulnerability scanning metrics green are baby steps to an overall goal where regulatory exams hold no surprises and decision-makers in risk analysis must justify decisions based on contribution to those goals. Ideally there should be consequences, such as performance bonus claw-backs, if cybersecurity program decisions turn out to be wrong. Note the practice of claw-backs has been used in various situations throughout the financial community (such as when traders attempt to drive up stock only until they sell), but it is not yet recognized as applicable to operational risk management. Of course, sympathetic consideration may be given to scenarios wherein managers inherit a chaotic state, and leeway may be provided due to recognized short-term influences. Perhaps other motivators (positive or negative) can be designed to encourage accountability for programs to grow the value of long-term capabilities over cosmetic improvements.

Recall the discussion in Chapter 7 about the cursory demonstration of compliance with a regulation by comparing it with words in an information security policy. Many cybersecurity executives used this approach when regulators first began asking questions about cybersecurity. By the time these same regulators became sophisticated enough to perform their own examinations, it was obvious these paper-based compliance demonstrations were not universally supported with sound underlying control processes. Regulator memos about matters requiring management attention and *immediate* management attention started to flow into financial institutions. At that time, the current cybersecurity executives were mostly able to blame their predecessors' judgment and point out that logically, the *Cybersecurity Program* did comply, even if the systems themselves did not then technically comply. This would be followed by agreement with the regulators that logically and technically are not the same thing. That said, an organization's technical plans to actually comply with regulations are typically measured in years, and this is sufficient time for a cybersecurity executive to have moved on to the next assignment, leaving his or her successor to explain why efforts may have fallen short of full compliance. Real plans for capability improvement need to consider criteria and testing for validation as part of the overall planning process.

Take Action Based on the Risk Assessment

To adopt the terminology of the NIST Cybersecurity Framework, an organization's cybersecurity posture is two-dimensional: *current* and *target*, or *as-is* and *to-be*. As depicted in Figure 8-3, improving the system that is vulnerable, not just by adding security components, can minimize residual risk. Cybersecurity improvements should be focused on reducing the vulnerability surface of the system under assessment, where system is understood to be composed of people, process, and technology.

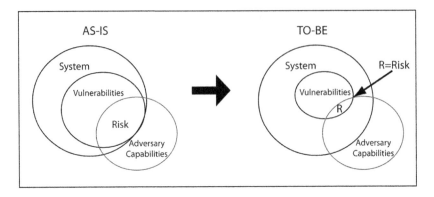

Figure 8-3. *Cybersecurity assessment result*

Mature cybersecurity programs are always improving as technology evolves; therefore, a set of issues that separates *as-is* from *to-be* is assumed to be ever-present. The key to making appropriate use of the situational awareness that comes with self-assessment is to make the most of the cyber capabilities to reduce vulnerabilities as quickly and effectively as possible, given the business objectives of the environment. This does not always mean deploying cybersecurity technology. Nevertheless, CISOs are sometimes tempted to tout cybersecurity program detection and response capabilities when simply eliminating vulnerabilities is within the same general cost and level of technology effort, though software engineers and/ or developers perform the tasks.

For example, in 2011, customer keys used in the RSA Security company's flagship product, the SecurID Card, were stolen from the vendor's network.[11] The SecurID Card was used for staff remote access by, among thousands of others, two major Department of Defense contractors: Lockheed Martin and Northrop Grumman.

1. Lockheed's cybersecurity group initiated an internal surveillance program designed to identify misuse of SecurID Cards. The team identified intruders using stolen RSA data to impersonate internal users with authorized access to the Lockheed network.

2.   Northrop Grumman's cybersecurity group
     immediately selected an alternative card vendor
     and replaced the vulnerable RSA SecurID cards with
     technology from the other vendor.

Some cybersecurity experts argued that Lockheed's approach was more sophisticated and technically harder for a security team to accomplish. However, Northrop Grumman suffered no successful attack attributed to the stolen data, and Lockheed Martin suffered reputational damage because their preventive security was technically breached due to a known vulnerability, even though they claimed no damage. In other words, in the cybersecurity community, it is no claim to fame to be the best at forensic investigation. It is far better to be invulnerable to attack.

Similarly, in the case of the 2017 Apache struts vulnerabilities, some financial institutions adopted a cybersecurity operations-centric approach. They set up sophisticated intrusion detection and automated response to try to thwart attempts at exploiting vulnerabilities. By contrast, other financial institutions with sophisticated software deployment organizations were agile enough to patch internet-facing services quickly with appropriate testing in tight timeframes, making the extended detection and automated response attempts to thwart the (continual) attacks unnecessary.

Build Situational Awareness

A full understanding of the sources of information used to prioritize risk and justify cybersecurity programs is the first step toward situational awareness. It enables us to actually manage cybersecurity risk. Businesses that pursue quality in any domain carefully select the measures of quality, and cybersecurity is no exception. What gets measured gets managed. The Information Technology Infrastructure Library (ITIL) has become the de facto reference for the professional practice of technology management.[12] The approach is to see that technology as a service is a set of detailed practices for IT service management (ITSM) and manage service levels accordingly. Incidents are items to be managed. Problems are incidents for which there is no current solution. The basic idea behind ITIL is to identify service parameters, measure them, and drive down defects. A caveat on using ITIL as a guide to cybersecurity is that when security is portrayed as a service, it becomes important to those performing the service to operate within service level agreements. For example, ITIL security services tend to be described as requirements for access to systems. This is not access control, it is actual access. Where security management adopts the mindset that they are in the business of giving access to people, this culture may create opposition to investigating why access is necessary. Consequently, service requests that should present problems to be investigated (e.g., *why does this person need access?*) are instead treated as incidents to be immediately resolved (e.g., *access must be provisioned within 1 day of the request*). Nevertheless, assuming that these conflicts can be resolved, and also that actual controls have attributes that are measureable (like the number of systems in inventory that are up to date on security patches), then following the ITIL approach to service quality is an easy way to begin measuring the quality of security as an element of the quality of the financial service it supports.

ITIL service targets are set in a manner very much like the Six Sigma approach to manufacturing quality, in which defects should be so scarce that the defect percentage of delivered product measurable unit is less than 0.000001 percent.[13] In both cases, management commitment to quality is reflected in the number of decimal places they are willing to target to achieve customer satisfaction. Cybersecurity controls are also typically measured with a sub-zero tolerance for failure in mind, and in practice, simple security controls like patching are often portrayed as requiring technology's equivalent of manufacturing quality, where tolerance for product defects results in immediate returns and financial losses, thus the adoption of Six Sigma.

Six Sigma uses a "5 Whys" technique to analyze metrics. The idea is to ask why a problem occurred, and when presented with the answer, ask again why that answer seems sufficient as explanation, and so on until the facts underlying the methodology used to quantify a result are clear to all who are expected to make decisions based on them. Whether or not a metric is green, risk managers and others in charge of oversight for the cybersecurity program should ask why they are meaningful to current management, and why acting in response to them is expected to improve the safety and soundness of the firm. In many firms, it may take more than 5 whys to create the transparency needed to fully explore the situation, but this is typically due to the inherent complexity of technology control environments.

When a "why" presents an unsolved cybersecurity problem, an executive faces a quality issue in a financial services operation. In such cases, there are tools and techniques that seem like obvious choices to consider. One is to gather data on the service in question and analyze it to look for patterns that lead to disappointing results. Risk assessment systems and/or GRC systems that use actual cybersecurity metrics should be seen as potential sources of data for quality analysis. They can be mined for potentially unexpected patterns in cybersecurity preparedness. Such data is one of the most important resources in the cybersecurity arsenal and is frequently overlooked. They are overlooked not only by risk analysts but also by line management, so often that a frequent audit finding in financial services is that computers are missing from the inventory from which GRC metrics are gathered.

To appreciate the value of high-level, or aggregate, metrics, think about the questions you have about the cybersecurity program, and see if the data can provide the answers. In devising metrics, it is helpful to use the 5-question technique, using the question, "How do you know?" For example, consider the case where the Target retail chain was compromised by attackers who entered via one of their data center support vendor's systems.[14] Suppose after the Target hack, a firm would like to find out whether they are vulnerable to that attack. Rather than ask a yes-or-no question, ask the CISO, "How can we measure our vulnerability to the Target attack?" The first response to the question would rely on whether the firm has records that show which network connections interface to third-party systems. Armed with that connectivity information, the second question is, "How do we know those connections cannot be used to infiltrate our networks?" This would require looking into network firewalls and traffic segregation filters to see if they limit vendor access to systems they maintain. The third question would be, "How do we know those systems cannot be used to harm our data confidentiality, integrity, or availability?" This would lead to measurement of sandbox controls on the systems to which they have access. Note that none of these questions have trivial answers, and most firms did not measure these controls in any systematic way that would have uncovered the Target attack before it occurred. Many that set out to answer those questions ended up adding several metrics to their security program before they could answer them in any reliable repeatable manner.

Figure 8-4. *The security team*

Conduct Realistic Drills, Tests, and Games

As stated earlier, cybersecurity is not a domain for the purely theoretical; it's only relevant when applied to real-world conditions. It is common to practice the execution of response and recovery tactics to demonstrate and test critical IT response capabilities. In the financial industry, regulators also require such demonstrations. The necessary investment for executing business continuity drills and penetration testing is maximized if the test scenarios closely resemble real events that have occurred in other firms and exploitation of hypothetical vulnerabilities in critical systems. Although this scenario selection goal may seem like common sense, there are three factors working against us in this regard: (1) sensitivity to costs, (2) fear of potential disruption, and (3) the inability to sufficiently account for circumstances vital to evaluation of test results, including technical architecture, business data streams, and human interactions under crisis.

Cost sensitivity is certainly a legitimate concern and needs to be balanced with all other potential cybersecurity investments; we can always expect to have limited budgets, and therefore funding requests should necessarily follow organizational budgeting practices. Therefore, the question each enterprise will need to answer is, "How much is testing worth?" Support for increasing emphasis, and spending, on testing that should be considered during budget decisions follows later in this section.

Fear of disruption frequently influences testing approaches because potentially negative risk effects from testing should certainly be considered. However, these can be minimized via standard risk treatment options such as avoidance—that is, highly sensitive architectures or operations can be excluded from the testing scope. Risk can also be reduced through approaches such as testing during non-business hours or only under the direct supervision of relevant technical subject matter experts. Risks of testing can be shared via test collaboration with business partners or even customers. And risk treatment options always include simply accepting the potential for negative outcomes, although the acceptance decision could prove operationally, if not politically, challenging.

Difficulties in sufficiently replicating real-world conditions are very apparent. This includes the practical inabilities to closely mirror technical architectures in our current era of large, massively distributed, diverse technology architectures. An increasing number of business data flows stem from very complex and distributed environments. For example, testing of trading desk or back office operations ideally should include the execution of test transactions passed at the velocity and volume experienced in the "production" environment. Although these problems are not insurmountable, they are challenging and may be expensive to simulate. Consideration of human interactions during a business disruption caused by a cyber attack opens an entirely new set of challenges. No one can easily predict how internal staff, trusted business partners, and customers will respond to learning of a suspected incident or to an actual service disruption. There clearly are legitimate causes for concern, and proper caution should be exercised in the planning and execution of drills and tests.

There are potential drivers that could push organizations toward inadequate tests and drills. These include concerns related to time, money, effort, and fear of disruption. Institutional avoidance of anything that requires expending resources certainly is understandable, and no responsible business leader should allow tests and drills that are perceived to have a real chance of damage to the enterprise. However, we have observed in practice indications that fear-uncertainty-and-doubt (commonly referred to as FUD) about potential disruptions from testing is alive and well inside some enterprises, and could water-down technical testing. Consider also the possibility some staff might favor narrow tests to avoid internal reputational damage if flaws gain visibility. Similarly managers, already in fierce battles for budgets, may not want the enterprise to shift even more funding toward cyber projects, and away from potential business innovations that could produce competitive advantage. For potential reasons such as these, planners of cybersecurity tests should therefore anticipate some level of hesitation might influence the development of testing scopes and "rules of engagement" (ROE).

The testing scope and ROE combine to set the operational constraints on the testing team. Commonly constrained aspects include approved testing dates and times, technical testing tools such as scanners, but could also include decisions such as marking entire sections of architecture "off limits" to testers. Such broad constraints could potentially raise questions of the rigor and legitimacy of the testing regime. It is not unreasonable to consider the possibility internal staff who are aware of substantial vulnerabilities might be tempted to place constraints in the scope and ROE to prevent the test team from coming near known problem areas, thereby avoiding detection. Similarly, constraints could potentially be designed to steer testing focus towards areas known to be robust, thereby drawing attention away from potential trouble spots. Test planners should therefore be ensured independence from operational staff so the planners can challenge testing limitations that appear overly restrictive. Planners could also document a clear rationale for all limitations so scoping decisions are recorded in the work papers and potentially described in the final report.

Due to these factors, there are three considerations vital to planning effective cybersecurity tests. First, organizations should strive to make their tests realistic. This includes mimicking the production environment as closely as possible using test systems and perhaps specialized architectures such as cyber test ranges. In some cases, organizations may find the only suitable testing approach is to conduct tests against all elements of the production architecture. Adversary conduct can be more closely replicated by relaxing the constraints commonly found in ROE. Second, organizations should consider fundamental, commonly accepted principles of controls design and testing. This should include ensuring the independence of the testing teams, so they are free from any form of interference or manipulation, intentional or otherwise. Third, it is crucial to build in feedback mechanisms throughout the test execution to allow effective socialization of findings to support the knowledge creation goals discussed previously.

Design of Technical Tests

Cybersecurity tests have their roots in the physical security concept of Design-Basis-Threat (DBT).[15] A DBT describes characteristics of the most powerful and innovative adversary that it is realistic to expect to protect against. In New York City, it may be a terrorist cell equipped with sophisticated communications and explosive devices. In Idaho, it may be a posse of vigilantes carrying machine guns on motorcycles. A DBT approach to security dictates that the strength of security protection required by a system is calculated with respect to a technical specification of how it is likely to be attacked. In physical security, this process is straightforward. If the DBT is a force of 20 people with access to explosives of a given type, then the strength of the physical barriers to unauthorized entry must withstand the ton of force that these 20 people could physically bring into system contact using those weapons. Barrier protection materials are specified, threat delay and response systems are designed, and validation tests are conducted accordingly. In cybersecurity, potential attacks are typically viewed as the aggregated set of all publicly documented cyber attacks to date, and these include threats that far exceed the design basis of financial industry standard penetration tests. In fact, it is often the case financial industry penetration testers are intentionally diffused as described previously.

Another challenge is that the scope of an adequate test cannot reasonably be accomplished by even the most sophisticated independent attack teams in a timeframe required to be included in an industry standard software deployment process. The industry standard repository for the set of all currently known vulnerabilities is the set of Common Vulnerabilities and Exposures (CVE)[16] in the National Vulnerability Database (NVD).[17] An automated scan for these vulnerabilities is designed to imitate the behavior of a malicious perpetrator, and the test's validity is based on its ability to predict how a system will withstand an attack.

Vulnerability test scores are assigned based on scan results. Security software that tests for such vulnerabilities usually uses a traffic light metric, wherein a system is rated *red* if it has any vulnerabilities that may be exploited to gain administrative access to the system, *yellow* if an exploit allows unauthorized access, and *green* if the system does not have any of the vulnerabilities included in the scan. However, some vulnerability scanning procedures use more sophisticated scoring methods, such as the Common Vulnerability Scoring System (CVSS).[18] CVSS evaluation includes a numeric score that is based on how easy it is for a perpetrator to accomplish significant damage by exploiting vulnerabilities. Systems that score high have vulnerabilities that are easily exploited, and those exploits can result in total system compromise. Regardless of the scoring system, each vulnerability is scored independently, and someone must decide in advance which vulnerabilities will be tested in a given system. As of this writing, the NVD contains 115,746 vulnerabilities. It also contains common misconfigurations and known software weaknesses that create common vulnerabilities that are not themselves CVEs. No system can or should be tested for all known vulnerabilities. Even if there was a practical way to identify which ones may be applicable to a financial institution's system, and to test those systems for all that apply, studies show that such vulnerability tests are fraught with both false-positives and false-negatives due to the difficulty of teams with diverse software tools designing and executing tests in multiple environments.[19]

It is important to consider tests that are based on vulnerability scanning only and test for vulnerabilities that are known. Yet the discovery of previously unknown threats is so routine that security professionals have a term for them, as described in chapter 2: zero-day threats.[20] There is no demonstrable connection between the number, or severity, of potential software vulnerabilities and the probability of cyber attack. Rather, studies have shown during the attack life cycle that the adversary's ability to discover security defects is dominated less by the intrinsic quality of the code and more by the time required to familiarize themselves with it.[21] So although it is important to check internally that software vulnerabilities do not exist, this is most efficiently and effectively done by internal teams who are thoroughly familiar with the code, not by people who are by design unfamiliar with it.

Tests as a method of calculating odds of being attacked therefore should be evaluated on two scales. The odds of being attacked and the odds of the attacker achieving objectives are two different things. A single exploited vulnerability may be construed as a successful attack, but if there is no damage to the confidentiality, integrity, or availability of the institution, its customers, or the financial system, the attacker has not achieved any objectives. In the cases where tests are conducted in non-production environments or halted prematurely, this second method of calculating odds may provide a false sense of security.

Move from Controls-Thinking to Capabilities-Thinking

Synonyms for "control" are "power," "rule," "restrain," and "limit." Those who have not spent time in control-oriented careers are naturally wary of such activities, and in some job functions, the very notion of control is tantamount to dictatorship. Control is commonly viewed as an impediment, a speed bump to productivity, and perhaps a barrier to innovation.

Individual and cybersecurity team professional development (i.e., knowledge creation) practices in areas such as cyber risk identification, vulnerability reduction, and risk measurement can help make cybersecurity risk more obvious to those who come to the field from purely technical backgrounds. Ideally organizations should promote a view that cybersecurity teams are respected members of the community of professional practitioners of financial services risk management. Where cybersecurity training is offered beyond IT or risk groups, those outside of the relative small circle of cybersecurity experts may find cybersecurity issues more obvious as well. Such recognition can foster accountability for issue ownership within business and technology operations outside of the core cybersecurity group.

In addition to conceptual training, we've noted there are also education benefits from participating in cybersecurity practice. This includes participation in the test scenarios previously described, and also in in-process operations such as patching, monitoring, and data analysis to support process improvement. For example, rotating cybersecurity and technology staff through cybersecurity assessment activities is one such form of practice. Any kind of realistic drills, tests, and other experiences with scenarios of account take-over, denial-of-service, data theft, and other frequently encountered financial industry cyber attacks that closely model real-world technical and business environments are good ways to gage overall competencies and effectiveness in executing the cybersecurity program. Such drills and practice turn experience into instinct and help staff understand the value of otherwise potentially daunting processes and procedures.

In the financial industry, it is also important to keep focused on the regulatory requirements related to cybersecurity capabilities, and the intended benefits from controls, ranging from the protection of specific IT assets to the integrity of financial transactions. Cybersecurity efforts should be positioned as foundational for such purposes. Note this is not the same as simple management support for a CISO to build and operate an information security program. That can evolve in many ways, some of which may be counter-productive. For example, there is a "fire-and-forget" form of management that is highly effective where individuals are provided with well-defined marketing methods to penetrate sales regions; they are thereafter noticed only if they are successful. This management style rarely works in control-oriented functions. Business leaders must be vigilant to make sure that the cybersecurity program does not become synonymous with the power of any single executive, no matter how financially successful, but instead continuously engage the entire executive team to establish control architectures they think will improve their capabilities to protect the enterprise from cyber attack.

Only once a cybersecurity program is sufficiently understood and respected will the rank and file take cybersecurity efforts, such as awareness training, seriously. Although there are regulatory requirements for cybersecurity and privacy training in most financial services jurisdictions, such programs tend to be relatively high level and focus on procedures such as issue escalation rather than professional development to support the learning goals described here.

All of the activities described in this chapter support the internal knowledge creation process for cybersecurity. There are external sources as well, including many professional industry organizations that share cybersecurity concerns, and professional best practices knowledge continuously improves through information sharing and industry socialization.[22] Both cybersecurity and non-cybersecurity staff should therefore be encouraged to join cybersecurity partnership organizations, private and public. The recognition of belonging to a community of interest with the clear responsibility to protect cyberspace is excellent motivation for a continually learning, and improving, cybersecurity program.

Moving Ahead

The process of building effective cybersecurity capabilities can be based on a foundation of knowledge sharing and organizational learning. This can be informed by the risk assessment but requires team activities such as realistic drills and tests to put cybersecurity operations and management through hypothetical scenarios that provide useful illustration of real-world decision-making considerations. The result is continuous improvement of skills, awareness, and overall preparedness.

The next chapter introduces the concept that, in addition to the use of planned drill and test activities, enterprises can draw potentially significant insights from actual cybersecurity event experiences, whether encountered by their own organization or another company. There can be substantial value, as explained in the next chapter, in learning from actual losses.

Notes

1. McKinsey & Company (2010) Building organizational capabilities: McKinsey Global Survey results.

    `https://www.mckinsey.com/business-functions/organization/our-insights/building-organizational-capabilities-mckinsey-global-survey-results`

2. Jansen, W., Directions in Security Metrics Research. 2009, National Institute of Standards and Technology Interagency Report.

3. Buede, Dennis M., *The Engineering Design of Systems, Models and Methods*. Hoboken, NJ: Wiley, 2009).

4. Morabito, Joseph, Sack, Ira, Bhate, Anilkumar. *Designing Knowledge Organizations: A Pathway to Innovation Leadership*. (Hoboken, NJ: Wiley, 2017).

5. Nonaka, Ikujiro and Takeuchi, Hirotaka. *The Knowledge-Creating Company*. (Oxford, UK: Oxford University Press, 1995).

6. See for example, the Financial Services Information Sharing and Analysis Center at: `https://www.fsisac.com/`

7. Hubbard, Douglas, *The Failure of Risk Management*, (Hoboken, NJ: Wiley, 2009).

8. National Institute of Standards and Technology (NIST), *Framework for Improving Critical Infrastructure Cybersecurity*, US Department of Commerce, 2014, page 3. *Note this topic has been significantly expanded in the latest draft revision.*

9. Factor Analysis of Information Risk (FAIR) Institute (2018) What is FAIR?. `http://www.fairinstitute.org/what-is-fair`, retrieved 3/11/18.

10. Hershfield, H. E., Cohen, T.R, & Thompson, L, "Short horizons and tempting situation: Lack of continuity to our future selves leads to unethical decision making and behavior, ." *Organizational Behavior and Human Decision Processes* 117(2): March, 2012, 298-310.

11. Drew, Christopher, "Stolen Data is Tracked to Hacking at Lockheed" *The New York Times*, June 3, 2011.

12. See `https://www.axelos.com/best-practice-solutions/itil`

13. Pande, Peter, et al., *The Six Sigma Way*, (New York: McGraw-Hill, 2001).

14. Krebs, Brian, "Target Hackers Broke in Via HVAC Company," in *Krebs on Security*,

    `https://krebsonsecurity.com/2014/02/target-hackers-broke-in-via-hvac-company/`

15.   Garcia, Mary Lynn, *The Design and Analysis of Physical Protection Systems*. (Oxford, UK: Butterworth-Heinemann, 2008).

16.   CVE is a registered trademark of The Mitre Corporation, see `https://cve.mitre.org/`.

17.   MITRE. National Vulnerability Database. ongoing; Available from: `http://nvd.nist.gov/`.

18.   Mell, P., K. Scarfone, and S. Romanosky, A Complete Guide to the Common Vulnerability Scoring System Version 2.0. 2007, Forum of Incident Response and Security Teams (FIRST).

19.   Fernandez, E.B. and N. Delessy. Using Patterns to Understand and Compare Web Services Security Products and Standards. in Proceedings of the Advanced International Conference on Telecommunications and International Conference on Internet and Web Applications and Services (AICT/ICIW 2006). 2006: IEEE.

20.   Acohido, Byron and Swartz, Jon. *Zero Day Threat*. (New York: Sterling Publishing Co., Inc, 2008).

21.   Clark, S., et al. (2014). Moving Targets: Security and Rapid-Release in Firefox. *Proceedings of the 2014 ACM SIGSAC Conference on Computer and Communications Security*. Scottsdale, Arizona, USA, ACM: 1256-1266.

22.   For example, see `www.isaca.org`, `www.isc2.org`, and `www.cisecurity.org`

CHAPTER 9

What Can We Learn From Losses?

Wisdom comes alone through suffering.

—Aeschylus, Tragedian

It is good for me that I was afflicted that I may learn Thy statutes.

—Psalms 119:71

Man cannot remake himself without suffering, for he is both the marble and the sculptor.

—Alexis Carrel, Nobel Prize winning scientist

What doesn't kill you makes you stronger.

—Kelly Clarkson, "Stronger (What Doesn't Kill You)" (2011)

This may very well be the first cybersecurity writing to connect thoughts from a Greek classic, the Bible, a Nobel Prize winner, and a pop star. The common thread through such diverse sources, however, is a very simple point–there has long been recognition of the benefit, perhaps need, for experiential learning, particularly when the underlying experiences are negative.

© Paul Rohmeyer, Jennifer L. Bayuk 2019
P. Rohmeyer and J. L. Bayuk, *Financial Cybersecurity Risk Management*,
https://doi.org/10.1007/978-1-4842-4194-3_9

Breaches Provide the Context That Standards Lack

The design of cybersecurity risk treatments can certainly be guided by available standards and prevailing common practices. Such an approach, however, can be inadequate without considering the context of specific, real-world breach event scenarios. Similarly, the integration of cybersecurity technologies without regard for context may provide generic prevention and detection capabilities, but without considering unique factors discovered in prior, actual breaches. So why do cybersecurity leaders often seem to overlook the enormous opportunity to use actual negative episodes to drive true organizational learning and, as a result, design better controls?

A clue comes from economist John Maynard Keynes who famously observed, "In the long run we are all dead."[1] This point may be somewhat harsh in the context of cybersecurity but the lesson is vital: learning takes time and effort and sometimes individual, pressured-filled drives to achieve short-term goals may occupy our attention. Benefits from learning in the present are often not realized until sometime in the future, and practical managers can rely on the fact that no one expects them to turn on a dime in response to negative events. Moreover, organizational forces can push leaders into short-term thinking, as decision-making is inevitably subject to internal power, politics, and sometimes consideration of career preservation. Nevertheless, a combined approach that achieves immediate cybersecurity benefits through the use of standards and available technologies along with a continuous process of analysis, study, and organizational learning may be the key to keeping pace with the continuing evolution of the threat environment. Standards, commercial software, and common practices reflect knowledge applied against known problems and clearly can provide substantial short-term benefits. Practiced organizational learning, however, can drive a complimentary capability to analyze dynamic, complex changes that require innovation. Innovation in the face of emerging threats is a vital component of cybersecurity resiliency.

Technology-Focused Resilience Is Just the Beginning

The term resilience has gained recent popularity with respect to cybersecurity. Resilience can be generally described as a capability to repel and/or bounce back from a negative event, and so the concept is somewhat of a natural fit in the cybersecurity realm. Information technology planners and auditors alike have been obsessed with the need for backup and recovery for years, and rightly so due to prior technological limitations. The advent of more naturally flexible and robust technology architectures opened the door for the progression from rudimentary backup/restore capabilities to more comprehensive architectural resiliency via advances such as cloud, virtualization, efficient data mirroring, and more.

The advance of technology in support of operational resiliency has been generally focused on economy and performance. For example, maintaining fully mirrored and cloud-hosted application data may eliminate the need for backup execution and media management with high degrees of personnel involvement, and therefore shorter fall-over timeframes. This certainly creates operational benefits, but it also illustrates a focus on tactical resiliency against general, perhaps likely, threats. A mirrored environment that experiences data corruption merely transfers the corruption to the backup platform faster than older technologies. Broadening the scope of resiliency study to include cybersecurity scenarios beyond individual component technical failures has the potential to lead the organization to take a more innovative enterprise perspective.

The Learning Organization Revisited

The prior chapter examined cybersecurity from the perspective of overall capabilities that include technology, process, and personnel dimensions. As technology resilience seems to have become a common organizational goal, process and personnel aspects appear to be drawing less attention than perhaps they should. Consideration of the concept of the learning organization as described earlier in this book provides clues on the potential for enterprises to use cycles of knowledge externalization, combination, internalization, and socialization to develop new organizational knowledge and therefore the capability to innovate. The process of knowledge creation holds a key to not only responding to prevailing threats but also to guiding the ongoing evolution and development of enterprise capabilities. There are numerous opportunities to support characteristics of the learning organization across many aspects of cybersecurity, including risk assessment, situational awareness, and cybersecurity testing.

The organizational learning processes can lead to better risk assessments, including supporting sharper recognition of threats and vulnerabilities as they could impact the unique characteristics of an enterprise. More importantly, the learning organization may be better positioned to take action as a result of risk assessment findings. Situational awareness entails the survey and analysis of a particular scenario and its environment in order to inform better decision making via the application of knowledge, and the learning organization can improve the chances the decision maker has relevant knowledge. Similarly, the design of cybersecurity tests can be approached with greater creativity and innovation when test planners have improved knowledge.

Capabilities can continuously improve based on the study of real-world events, including actual painful episodes. This includes breaches that have damaged the enterprise as well as potentially other organizations with similar operational characteristics. In other words, we can use the negative experience of breaches to enable deeper study of threats and vulnerabilities, thereby improving organizational cybersecurity knowledge and driving innovation across the enterprise cybersecurity architecture.

Easier Said Than Done

If suffering brings wisdom, I would wish to be less wise.

—William Butler Yeats, Poet

It's not always pleasant and it's not always easy to learn from bad experiences. In the book, *The Up Side of Down: Why Failing Well Is the Key to Success*, author Megan McArdle illustrates psychological dimensions associated with individuals' attitudes and therefore responses to failure.[2] Our perceptions of what it means to be smart, successful, and respected can present significant barriers to developing a mindset that we can and must learn from failure despite the personal discomfort and, in the organizational context, potential damage to personal reputation from being individually labeled something of a "failure" due to a cybersecurity-related loss event. Cyber risk, like risk from physical crime, will never be eliminated, and so even the best prepared organizations can experience a breach. The opportunity lies in learning so that we can somehow benefit from the negative episode.

It is always a struggle to be objective in our observations of an internal event, and subsequently model said event in order to confirm our understanding as best as possible. The use of a particular breach event as the basis for a model to guide decision making in the design of controls (and tests of controls) is certainly helpful but may be imperfect. Nassim Taleb described the concept of the "ludic fallacy" in his book, *The Black Swan*. Taleb explained attempts to model real-world challenges using past events and games will always be imperfect, as we can rarely acquire complete information about the past event, and game scenarios are by nature limited. Taleb also noted the potential for tiny variations to create substantial problems in our attempts to model complex scenarios. This means that the resulting model does not include potential outcomes that could possibly have happened as the event unfolded, but yet did not.[3]

So while using past cyber events as templates can potentially improve our controls design and testing, we should understand that we are likely to miss something that may be very meaningful. For example, we clearly cannot expect to duplicate all of the characteristics and conditions that existed in the environment of the adversary's preparation of the known, prior attack in order to repeat the same attack scenario in a cyber game against an internet-facing application. In addition, Taleb noted games are subject to limitations (i.e., game rules), while the real world has no such limitations. This aside, the prevalence of cyber games in today's cybersecurity education systems reflects an assumption that we could potentially construct a useful cybersecurity game (test) using the available information. While such games are no doubt useful training tools, hopefully our knowledge of our own systems environment, in combination with our understanding that all models are wrong even though some are useful,[4] will help us develop credible tests and games that are beneficial despite likely imperfections.

AntiFragile

Taleb followed the *Black Swan* with *Antifragile–Things That Gain From Disorder,* another book that is particularly relevant to the current state of cybersecurity. In *Antifragile*, Taleb enumerated common reactions to uncomfortable events, which include *overreaction*, using *stressors as information*, and *lecturing birds how to fly*.

Our natural tendency to *overreact* in response to uncomfortable scenarios drives innovation. Recalling the Roman senator Cato who observed comfort as a "road to waste," Taleb recounted how the FAA observed that increased automation in airplanes may have had an eroding effect on pilot skill.[5] It's not too far a leap to consider the same negative effect may apply to cybersecurity, as enterprises invest in increasingly sophisticated cyber tools that may in turn cause cyber operators to have less opportunity, and perhaps less motivation, to take a deep dive into potential breaches. In some cases, overreaction may lead to the deployment of redundant control layers. Taleb also observed a tendency towards this type of redundancy in natural systems. However, operators in enterprises with relatively low investment in cyber tools face potential breaches with a natural panic (perhaps excitement) as they struggle to overcome observational and data challenges to diagnose an unfolding event. It is the uncertainty in spite of available tools that provides a source of motivation to drive intensive study.

This highlights a related observation that observations or indicators pushing us outside of our comfort zones represents, at the very least, a signal worthy of investigation. Taleb's concept of stressors as information[6] can be related to the cybersecurity context as alerts, event reports, threat intelligence, breach reports from other organizations, unexpected system performance, changes to the physical environment in the case of cyber-physical systems, and practically anything else that hints of disorder. It is just these sorts of indicators that can motivate cybersecurity leaders to investigate. It is precisely the uncomfortable nature of the pain/disorder/disruption that drives technology and business management into investigation and analysis. Therefore, mechanisms to notice potential stressors become essential in order to gain from negative forces and events. As information encourages us to consider signals that are accompanied by greater explanation (i.e., context) it is the relatively richer indicators that ideally should inform decision-making and, ultimately, drive changes to existing systems and processes, rather than layering on new ones.

It is important to note most of the concepts and examples presented in this book are almost entirely derived from, or refined via, the professional practice of cybersecurity risk management. Although we have deep empathy for our colleagues in academia, the field is too new to find value in any study of the efficacy of cybersecurity tools and techniques without complementary, practical application. Taleb describes the flow of scientific theory building as moving from academia to application and eventually to common practice. With dry humor, he provides an example of a progression from vector mathematics to the development of theories of ornithological navigation, and so on, eventually resulting in birds flying. Taleb dryly noted birds are unable to tell us their views on the subject, and then presented an alternative flow of problem-solving progression that starts with "random tinkering," processes followed by the development of associated heuristics and technology, and ultimately practical application.[7]

In *The Coming Storm*, Michael Lewis describes the professional practice of weather as very immature at the time when it was most needed, during World Wars I and II. He writes that the demand for weather forecasting was so high that the supply had no choice but to make a fraudulent appearance.[8] There is an analogy here with cybersecurity in that the field is full of products that appear to be random tinkering of questionable value for the purpose of cybersecurity risk reduction. But there is optimism it will ultimately yield practical application, as described by Taleb.

This progression of course aligns with the prior chapter's exploration of the learning organization. Cybersecurity analysis would be largely theoretical, and therefore inadequate, unless the capabilities were informed by the continuous experience of actual loss events (i.e., discomfort or damage) over time. Feedback loops from real-life experiences are therefore essential to the learning process.

Learn, Study Mistakes, and Learn Again

Observers of cybersecurity challenges often lament the continuous evolutions of the space as a result of numerous complex, dynamic, and simultaneous drivers. You may have referred to this at times as a "treadmill" or "hamster wheel" scenario, from which there is no escape.[9] Cycles of discovery via experiencing a painful/loss episode, followed by investigations and analysis, and ultimately corrective action are followed by more of the same. In the financial industry, it is not uncommon for new cyber incident response organizations to be formed as a knee-jerk reaction to a cybersecurity event. Unfortunately this sometimes occurs even without adequate consideration of how the enterprise will continue normal, ongoing operations. Along with this cycle comes substantial concerns with resource consumption, whether it is recognition that cybersecurity is consuming an increasing share of budgets, as well as disdain for the way cybersecurity breaches can essentially take over an organization's agenda until resolved.

The same can be said, however, of other organizational processes. In sales, adversaries are market competitors that continuously devise (innovate) new ways to undermine the competitor's credibility and steal customers. The factors are very similar–information is a stressor whether it is notice of a breach or a report of dipping sales, and the stressors lead to innovation. So what's the difference with cybersecurity that causes it to be approached differently than business problems? Why is cybersecurity sometimes not prioritized at the executive level? There are a few potential factors. First, cybersecurity is obviously not the core business of most organizations, and so the discussion of cybersecurity typically will not be approached with the same vigor as organizational strategy. Second, the dynamics of cybersecurity commonly entail a degree of technical complexity that can perhaps overwhelm relatively non-technical leaders. Third, there is common suspicion that controls applied in the name of cybersecurity risk management can unintentionally stifle organizational flexibility and innovation along with it.

Moving Ahead

As presented throughout this book, enterprises cannot be effective in cybersecurity without individual and organizational commitments to continuous learning to drive ongoing architectural improvement, and it needs to be fueled by reality. Bad experiences are higher octane than incremental feedback from risk assessments, audits, and the over-constrained penetration test.

Execution of this vision can be aided by introducing more focus on errors into oversight functions, such as increasing formality via a DAT (Defect Analysis Team) from the annals of Total Quality Management, or DMAIC (Define, Measure, Analyze, Improve and Control) process from Six Sigma.[10] Even rudimentary discussions of root causes could provide the platform to capture key learning from observed loss events. Plainly visible characteristics of loss events, including adversary techniques, methods, and evidence, can serve as important clues that ideally should cause the organization to question their own control assumptions and perhaps make their own cybersecurity controls testing strategies more consistent with prevailing adversary tactics.

However, before implementing a new DAT or DMAIC process, leaders can perhaps best start the process of becoming less fragile with some basic questions. When the news of the latest breach event hits the media, think about how the CISO, CRO, and CAO are able to illustrate how the existing controls environment theoretically protects the enterprise from experiencing the exact same fate as the damaged organization. Then consider whether the organization has evidence to prove it.

In the next and final chapter we will consider the impact of these factors on the emerging internal and external environments. New, innovative technology trends have the potential to further increase the importance of enterprise learning about the nature of upcoming innovations and the potential for new adversary tactics to exploit new technical vulnerabilities as industry tries to keep pace.

Notes

1. Keynes, John Maynard. *A Tract on Monetary Reform*, ch. 3. p. 80. (London Macmillan and Co., 1923). The Richest Man in Babylon, ISBN-13: 978-1607960812

2. McArdle, Megan. *The Up Side of Down: Why Failing Well is the Key to Success.* (London: Penguin Books, 2014). ISBN-13: 978-0143126362

3. Taleb, Nassim Nicholas. *The Black Swan: The Impact of the Highly Improbable.* (New York: Random House, 2007). ISBN-13: 978-0812973815

4. Box, George, (1976), "Science and Statistics" (PDF), *Journal of the American Statistical Association*, 71: 791–799.

5. Taleb, Nassim Nicholas. *Antifragile – Things That Gain From Disorder.* (New York: Random House, 2012). ISBN-13: 978-0812979688. pp. 41-45.

6. Taleb, Nassim Nicholas. *Antifragile – Things That Gain From Disorder.* (New York: Random House, 2012). ISBN-13: 978-0812979688. pp. 56-59.

7. Taleb, Nassim Nicholas. *Antifragile – Things That Gain From Disorder.* (New York: Random House, 2012). ISBN-13: 978-0812979688. pp. 194-197.

8. Lewis, Michael, *The Coming Storm*, Audible.com, July 31, 2018.

9. Jaquith, Andrew, *Security Metrics*, (London: Pearson Education, 2007), p. 3.

10. DMAIC in Six Sigma. Villanova University. Retrieved from `https://www.villanovau.com/resources/six-sigma/six-sigma-methodology-dmaic/#.WuSFri-ZPWU`

CHAPTER 10

So What's Next?

In the past century, each generation has created new technology that existed only in science fiction for the previous generation. These new technologies are then quickly taken for granted as innovation continues. Although it is not easy to forecast the future in a rapidly changing landscape where there is no analogous statistical history on which to draw, there are industry leaders who are changing today's landscape in ways that make it easier to see where the flow of progress is taking us. There are two vital dimensions to the flow of evolution in financial systems: progress in financial services and progress in financial services technology.

Complexity and Interconnectedness

Growth in the financial industry had been relatively quiet since the 2008 US financial crisis. While the investigations and new safety and soundness rules were underway, US regulators established an unofficial moratorium on new bank charters. This changed in 2017, with some new charter applications being approved. This trend may open the door for financial services to evolve as the financial technology companies (fintechs) have in the years in between, to tout innovations in technology as competitive differentiators. That said, there has been more progress in banks outside of the US providing innovative fintech services.

© Paul Rohmeyer, Jennifer L. Bayuk 2019
P. Rohmeyer and J. L. Bayuk, *Financial Cybersecurity Risk Management*,
https://doi.org/10.1007/978-1-4842-4194-3_10

Fintech is a new technology category used to provide a financial services but, at least in the US, may not be subject to specific regulatory or licensing requirements. The currency underlying a fintech transaction is often a credit card, and such fintech services often include peer-to-peer payments. These are usually provided via an online or mobile software application that allows an individual to charge their credit card to transfer money into another individual's online or mobile account. Then the second individual can transfer that money out of their fintech account into a bank account via an automated clearing house (ACH) transfer. Other fintech services collaborate directly with banks or brokerage services to front-end a banking, brokerage, or insurance service to cultivate communities of similarly minded customers, enhance the user experience, and create social networks.

A growing number of fintechs diverge complete from traditional banking assets and instead base transactions on one or more cryptocurrencies. Cryptocurrency fintechs provide an alternative to the traditional financial system based on a digital representation of money that has no value in the (US) licensed banking systems.[1] These are typically implemented with ledgers that start with some amount of digitally represented currency and a set of transactions that allow people to invest in the cryptocurrency with traditional currency, and/or participate in a market that enables online transactions. Records of cryptocurrency ownership are available to all market participants via a ledger system that may be centrally managed and/or distributed among the owners. In most cases, there is also some method of maintaining balances or cryptokeys that unlock ownership records locally on personal machines. Cryptocurrency fintechs offer to exchange traditional currency for an account in a ledger shared with other digital currency holders. There is no state-sponsored guarantee that the currency holds value apart from the perception of the community that participates in the market.

The "crypto" in the word cryptocurrency (or cryptocoin) is a reference to a blockchain or other cryptographic algorithm used to verify the integrity of the coin's ledger. A common necessary attribute of cryptocoin is that a well-defined algorithm provides a method of establishing the integrity of a source of a digital ledger entry. These verify that a ledger entry is a product of some computation based in part on the value of an original "seed" ledger entry of the digital currency. Cryptographic algorithms are used to document the transfer of ownership from one individual user to another, and so the chain of transactions can be recomputed at any time to verify that a coin is authentic.

Note that because fintech services powered by credit cards still either pay merchant fees for credit card transactions, and/or fintech services are backed by ACH transfers, traditional banks may still make money from fintech transactions. Consequently, in some respects fintechs who are not banks are not necessarily bank competitors; rather they can be valuable sources of new types of banking customer transactions. The future challenge will be for traditional banks to catch up with the financial services digital fintech customers are starting to expect. The new age of digital banking is expected to be a deep dive into the emerging world of seamless online socially aware financial services.[2]

This challenge has been echoed by the US Federal Reserve and other institutions who call for innovations in technology to cover inadequacies in the traditional banking systems, such as serving "underbanked" populations and the high cost of fraud borne by merchants. For example, the US Federal Reserve has proposed five "desired outcomes" that could benefit payment systems within a decade: [3]

1. Speed, ubiquity, and low-cost payment clearing and settlement;

2. Security designed to combat emerging threats;

3. Efficiency in the form of increased automation;

4. International settlements services that are timely, convenient, and cost-effective; and

5. Collaboration among a broad array of payment participants, including banks and merchants working together to achieve material progress on the first four outcomes.

The US Federal Reserve has been specific about the need for the financial industry to adopt high-speed networks, mobile technologies, and real-time transactions between individuals and businesses. Moreover, it expects real-time payments to work through mobile devices. It has also identified opportunities for expansion of the National Settlement Service, which allows financial institutions to exchange and settle transactions with businesses through master accounts held at the Federal Reserve. Tone at the top of this nature, in combination with customer expectations for more sophisticated services, makes progress in banking systems seem assured. Like Smart Order Routing innovations in the Securities Industry in the early 2000s, ubiquitous payment technology is expected to evolve to allow a bank to automatically identify and execute any given transaction at the lowest cost for the customer. Customers should be able to set payment preferences that override the lowest cost, such as a preferred reward points issuer or faster access to funds by the payee. These innovations are expected to create transparency between competitive payment networks that will allow discerning customers to understand the value of a payment routing system that places priority on their interests.

New financial service features are expected not only to put the interests of the payer first, but also to consider accounts, transactions, payment strategies, and third-party integration strategies as multiple dimensions of customer-centric digital transaction architecture. The complexity is expected to be seamless from the perspective of increasingly more digital-literate consumers. These include un-banked and under-banked young people that are paying monthly fees for simple banking services that come free with more privileged accounts. New services are expected to allow them to pay per transaction to avoid flat monthly fees. These consumers are expected to be able to take advantage of new low-cost payments delivered by efficient technology architectures at a fraction of the costs they pay today and to have access to easily understood personal ledgers that show them how much they are paying for their financial services. Such transaction-based service offerings are also expected to help community banks that may not currently participate in peer-to-peer payment systems due to high costs of entry.

Access to data on transactions is expected to extend to merchants who partner with banks on credit card offerings. In the foreseeable future, merchants should be able to estimate costs of direct participation in competitive peer-to-peer networks by reviewing aggregated customer transaction patterns. That is, new financial services technology will yield a competitive advantage whereby consumers and merchants will more easily be able to establish relationships directly with each other, rather than both remaining passive participants in the relatively anonymous interaction using today's ubiquitous credit card services (Figure 10-1).

Figure 10-1. *Looking ahead*

Potential Cybersecurity Implications

Predicting the future for cybersecurity is a multifaceted proposition. Some focus predictions on the spectrum of future threats. This is explored in a well-covered landscape of literature, some based on the expectation of increasing numbers of current cybersecurity incidents[4] and some based on current knowledge of known vulnerable technologies that have not yet been exploited.[5] Those who view the world through the lens of threats are growing increasingly anxious about the lack of regulation in cyberspace, much the same way the activists in the early 1900s grew increasingly concerned about industrial revolution's impact on rivers and streams.[6] Some focus on potential technology industry responses to the growing volume of threatening statistics like the increasing costs of damages due to cybercrime and the increasing ubiquity of cyber targets. These concerns typically lead to predictions for growth in the cybersecurity tools and/or employment marketplace.[7] To be cynical, such predictions are very often made by cybersecurity industry participants who will undoubtedly profit from increases in cybersecurity spending. Nevertheless, the steady growth in cybersecurity spending is just as assured as the growth in spending on water quality testing was in the early 1900s.[8]

The implications for the financial industry are clear to the extent improvements in cybersecurity posture are necessary. However, there is little consensus on exactly what improvements are expected. The challenges presented by the increased size and scope of the financial systems environment include ever-expanding connectivity between multiple types of stakeholders, and thus opportunities for account takeovers, insider fraud, and ransomware attacks. As successful enterprises enter the future and strengthen the financial systems infrastructure in ways that will make it more serviceable to consumers and businesses, these developments will necessitate major innovations in cybersecurity. Some of these innovations may be in pilot mode at this time, but none have reached the status of a new paradigm. Just as physical environmental impact studies are now a primary planning consideration for new manufacturing plants, a similar perspective is needed to provide cybersecurity assurance for new technologies.

The ever-more devastating cyber attacks of the past decade, in combination with the increasing dependency on automation in every industry, has caught the attention of every governance–themed organization from the National Association of Corporate Directors (NACD) to the National Institute of Standards and Technology (NIST). NACD acknowledges that standalone board agenda items on cybersecurity are prevalent but not adequate and calls for integration of cybersecurity in full board discussions on strategy.[9] NIST acknowledges cybersecurity management to date has been primarily operational and emphasizes that for such programs to be effective, management must ensure that cybersecurity is factored into enterprise risk considerations.[10] All governance advice on cybersecurity emphasizes that cybersecurity controls are essential to reduce enterprise risk, and governance questions are increasingly focused on the potential impact on mission should cybersecurity controls be subverted. As this progression extends to technology controls generally, the financial services and other industries become increasingly dependent on data and computational integrity controls to support the risk management process itself.[11]

Investments in modern transaction processing technology and cybersecurity are important for risk mitigation, but increased automation in general may also increase the probability that high-frequency, low-severity losses may transform into low frequency, high-severity losses. As the Bank of International Settlements has warned, automation does not have to be internal to impact risk but may be associated with loss or extended disruption of external services caused by external events.[12] For example, a cyberattack on a telecommunications provider is beyond the control of the financial industry, but analysis of undersea cable vulnerabilities provides a good example of how financial services are dependent on other industries to deliver financial transactions, and are themselves vulnerable due to this dependency.[13] Financial institutions must recognize that both internal and external cybersecurity incidents could jeopardize their ability to process transactions.

As interconnectedness becomes more and more ubiquitous, customers may be identified via internal customer directory lookup, e-mail addresses that correspond to customer or a customer of a connected payments network, a bank routing and account number, a merchant identifier (via a payments system service utilizing Near Field

Communication (NFC) or Quick Response (QR) Code enabled via a mobile device), a VISA/MasterCard/Amex or other credit card number, a fintech account, and/or another Financial Institution's Peer-to-Peer (P2P) payments service. As these become trusted sources for payment routing, identity itself may become a more competitive service. For example, e-mail service providers may be expected to collaborate with banks to compete for consumers based on cybersecurity features that prevent account takeover via e-mail password reset techniques.

Emerging Standards

Corporate functions in financial institutions will no doubt continue to require internet access to communicate with counterparties, vendors, and service providers. But in response to cyber threats, these internet connections will be constrained via ever-narrowing funnels provided by sandbox technology that restricts internet access to specific transaction-related use cases. Many new fintech-like services will be designed with cybersecurity as a primary consideration, and so even when operated by banks, new payment systems and other new financial services platforms may operate separately and independently from a financial institution's core support functions. Customer service access to data may be expected to be increasingly limited and monitored, reducing opportunities for insider-aided data loss events. Financial services operations may be expected to communicate with customers and third-party banking service providers only via tightly configured protocols that accept only authorized and encrypted communications. Data flows will be customized for each counterparty, allowing only small sets of agreed-upon data records to pass between systems.

Such collaboration may be based in part on security standards established for financial top-level internet domains that end in ".bank". The ".bank" top-level domain is a recent addition to the internet registry for the purpose of reducing the risk of cyber attacks that mimic a financial services domain. Only banks who meet all the security standards are considered for inclusion in this domain, as set forth by the fTLD Registry Services, LLC, a financial services industry consortium.[14] These standards include independent security reviews, e-mail authentication, and multifactor authentication for changes to the bank's registration information.

As the theme of standard financial cybersecurity measures is applied to the fintech model of optimizing bank technology systems, new data structures may be expected to be designed to more easily integrate with other financial institutions. This is a core requirement of US Sheltered Harbor, which ensures that customer data is preserved in an air-gapped data vault, in an immutable standard data format that may be recovered and serviced by qualified restoration service providers.[15] As the number of cyberattacks rise, more banks will feel pressure to join Sheltered Harbor as both affected participants and restoration providers.

Another relatively recent development is the expectation that a major financial institution's cybersecurity support system should meet the specifications for Qualified Anti-Terrorism Technology (QATT) set forth in the Department of Homeland Security's Safety Act.[16] Although the design objectives for QATT were originally envisioned for technology products, they were written to ensure that cybersecurity systems will smoothly integrate policies, procedures, technologies, and services. A benefit of certified QATT standards compliance is certain protections for claims arising from the performance or non-performance of the seller's QATT in relation to an act of terrorism. This motivated Bank of America to propose that their Critical Infrastructure Protection and Security Services be considered a QATT. The Bank of America QATT is described as "an integrated security system consisting of policies, procedures, services and component systems designed to provide a centralized capability to assess changing threat conditions and activities which could pose a threat to the bank's enterprise and to take actions to mitigate and respond to such risks."[17] It also encompasses services performed by Bank of America Corporation's Protective Services Group and Security Operations Analysis and Command Center (SOACC). This proposal was accepted and the bank's technology has been on the QATT list since March 2013. Other banks are expected to follow this example. The result will be testable capability to continually assess and respond to evolving cyber attacks that could pose a threat to financial services and/or customer operations and assets.

Not surprisingly, the QATT list also includes several cybersecurity risk assessment systems. These are a broad class of technologies that range from pure cybersecurity tools, such as automated penetration tests, to traditional "checklist" aids for oversight, referred to as "Governance, Risk, and Control" (GRC) systems. Increasingly, vendors are integrating regulatory compliance checklists into these tools, and the "C" in GRC is understood to refer to "Compliance" with both internal policies and external regulatory and industry standards. It is fast becoming industry standard to align or map internal policies with cybersecurity standards and regulations so that changes in internal control procedures can easily be reviewed for impact, both positive and negative, on cybersecurity maturity from a regulatory perspective. These tools and techniques may be expected to consolidate more and more standards and facilitate convergence on best practices via demonstrable utility of sets of controls in thwarting cyber attacks.

As cybersecurity risk management tools mature, similarities between cybersecurity team toolkits and traditional risk management tools will become more obvious and converge. For example, cybersecurity managers have long been vocal proponents of "tabletop exercises," while traditional financial service risk managers are proponents of "scenario analysis." These are both exercises in hypothetical situations and, when automated, can easily be consolidated into the same type of data structures and interfaces. The difference is that the financial risk management tools have been, to use a colloquial industry term, "regulatory-required" to use actual financial statements and credit portfolios to demonstrate the integrity of their models, whereas information technology risk assessments have been more subjective. The future will see cybersecurity measurement tools increasing in sophistication, and interfacing with financial institution technology management platforms and intrusion prevention systems to ensure that cybersecurity standards are demonstrably followed throughout the full technology life cycle for all systems that support financial services.

This will break some of the current silos in the cybersecurity assessment process, reducing the number of cases where assessments are paper exercises or questionnaires. The cybersecurity community resorts to questionnaires to ensure assessments are as complete as possible, but in reality the questionnaire method tends to have the opposite effect because the individuals filling out the questionnaires tend to be less technical and not likely to challenge those who actually operate cybersecurity technology. They are also often more junior than the cybersecurity managers who own the control processes undergoing assessment, and often work in a different department. So rather than seek ways to identify and measure the correctness and effectiveness of controls cited in assessment questionnaires, they often interview the cybersecurity practitioners who operated them and transcribe their responses. The silo effect allows the cybersecurity practitioners plausible deniability in being inaccurately assessed because the difficulty of exactly matching a question to the business environment is usually the responsibility of the assessor.

As cybersecurity assessment tools come of age, it will be more and more difficult for there to be plausible deniability of cybersecurity issues among the governance committees and boards that have oversight for financial services technology. When issues of regulatory non-compliance may be systematically reported via ubiquitous software, there may be more serious implications for negligence with respect to cybersecurity controls.

The scrutiny with which financial services industry cybersecurity risk management is judged can only be expected to increase. Certainly, cybersecurity programs that are fully integrated with banking operations may be expected to endure such scrutiny, and these are increasingly systemic operations that cross the boundaries of individual institutions and the third-party service providers that cater to the industry. Of course, since Sarbanes Oxley, firms have already expected to be able to demonstrate that cybersecurity programs are effective with well-defined and measurable processes and technology, but the number of counterparties instituting security requirements is increasing. For example, the largest global provider of secure financial messaging services, SWIFT, has established a Customer Security Program wherein they have published a "Customer Security Controls Framework" that includes a set of cybersecurity controls that are mandatory for SWIFT customers.[18] Customers are required to attest that these controls are in place; presumably, those who do not face potential exclusion from the SWIFT network.

In summary, these expectations should lead to increased transparency in financial services cybersecurity control mechanisms, which in turn should provide a degree of confidence that customer and regulatory expectations for cybersecurity are adequately met. And where it is found that expectations for cybersecurity are not met, this increased transparency should at least provide assurance that the financial services industry is fully committed to (1) improved situational awareness to the changing threat landscape; (2) corresponding evolution in protection mechanisms; and (3) strengthened attack response. No bank is an island, and when the bell of cybersecurity attack tolls, it tolls for all.[19]

Notes

1. That is, except that gains are considered taxable income. For an overview of country policy with respect to cryptocurrencies, see, `https://www.investopedia.com/articles/forex/041515/countries-where-bitcoin-legal-illegal.asp`

2. Skinner, Chris, Digital Bank, Strategies to Launch or become a Digital Bank, Marshall Cavedish, 2014, pp. 227-228.

3. Federal Reserve System, "Strategies for Improving the US Payments System (2015)" and "Federal Reserve Next Steps in the Payments Improvement Journey (2017)," see `http://fedpaymentsimprovement.org`

4. For example: Goodman, Marc, *Future Crimes*, (New York: Anchor, 2015, reprinted 2016).

5. For example: P.W. Singer and August Cole, *Ghost Fleet*, (Boston: Eamon Dolan/Mariner Books, 2015, reprinted 2016).

6. See Carlson, Rachel, *Silent Spring*, (New York: Houghton Mifflin, 1962).

7. Morgan, Steve, "Top 5 cybersecurity facts, figures and statistics for 2017." *CSO Online* - `www.csoonline.com`, October 19, 2017

8. Bradley, Tony, "Gartner Predicts Information Security Spending To Reach $93 Billion In 2018." *Forbes*, August 17, 2017.

9. Clinton, Larry, *Cyber-Risk Oversight, Director's Handbook Series*, National Association of Corporate Directors, 2017, p. 10.

10. National Institute of Standards and Technology, Framework for Improving Critical Infrastructure Cybersecurity, US Department of Commerce, draft update 2016, section 4.

11. Bayuk, Jennifer, "Technology's Role in Enterprise Risk Management." *ISACA Journal*, Volume 2, 2018.

12. Basel Committee on Banking Supervision (2003) *Sound Practices for the Management and Supervision of Operational Risk*. p.11.

13. US Department of Homeland Security, Threats to Undersea Cable Dependency, September 28, 2017, https://www.dni.gov/files/PE/Documents/1---2017-AEP-Threats-to-Undersea-Cable-Communications.pdf, retrieved 8/16/2018.

14. See https://www.ftld.com

15. See https://shelteredharbor.org/

16. See https://www.safetyact.gov/

17. See entry for Bank of America on the "Approved Technologies" list at: https://www.safetyact.gov/lit/at/aa

18.   SWIFT Customer Security Controls Framework,
       see `https://www.swift.com/myswift/`
       `customer-security-programme-csp_/security-`
       `controls/2019`, retrieved 8/16/2018.

19.   Reference by analogy to: "No man is an island", a
       line from: Devotions upon Emergent Occasions,
       John Donne, 1624.

Index

A

Acceptance, risk, 114–115
Advanced persistent
  threat (APT), 7
Adversary, cyber threats
 insider *vs.* outsider
  perspectives, 4
 intentional/unintentional
  actions, 4
 lack of data, 3
 OWASP, 5
 skill levels, 5
 typology of, 5
Antelope metaphor, 122
Antifragile, 228
Apache Struts vulnerability, 83,
  88–89, 93
Application support team, 64
Attackers, 24
Automated clearing
  house (ACH), 236
Automated Teller Machine (ATM)
  services, 170
 attacks, 171
 bank clients, 170
 Channel owner, 176
 data transfer and message
  sequence integrity, 170

 fraud, 173
 information, 171
 internal control, Banks, 175
 security
  responsibilities, 173–175
 shared industry networks, 170
 transaction flow, 171, 173

B

Bank of International Settlements
  (BIS), 54
Breach
 calculation, 54
 cost estimate, 65–68, 70
 cybersecurity, 50–51, 53–54, 62
 impact analysis, 52
 loss categories, 54–55
 risk, 49
 scenario
  creation, 55–57
  selection, 58–59
Business E-mail Compromise
  (BEC)
 controls, 34
 identification of
  attack, FBI, 32–33
 process dimensions, 33

© Paul Rohmeyer, Jennifer L. Bayuk 2019
P. Rohmeyer and J. L. Bayuk, *Financial Cybersecurity Risk Management*,
https://doi.org/10.1007/978-1-4842-4194-3

W, X, Y, Z

Printed in the United States
By Bookmasters